THE FIRST SQUARE

JACK RANDALL

First published in Great Britain in 2024 by Pensax Publishing

Text copyright © Jack Randall, 2024

Foreword copyright © Tim Jones, 2024

Design and typesetting by Orphans Press Ltd.

The rights of Jack Randall to be identified as the Author of the Work has been asserted by him in accordance with the Copyright, Design and Patents Act 1988. All rights reserved.

No part of this publication may be reproduced, stored in a retrieval system or transmitted, in any form or by any means, electronic, mechanical, photocopying, recording or otherwise, without the prior written permission of the publisher.

A Cataloguing in Publication record for this book is available from the British Library.

ISBN: 978-1-399991-19-3

Printed and bound by Orphans Press Ltd, Herefordshire HR6 0LD

CONTENTS

Acknowledgements 1

The First Square – Foreword by Tim Jones,
Worcestershire CCC Club Historian 3

Chapter One: My boyhood interest in cricket 5

Chapter Two: Early Cricket in the County 11

Chapter Three: The First-Class County 20

Chapter Four: 1929 - 1939 32

Chapter Five: The 1940's and 1950's 41

Chapter Six: 1960 - 1970 57

Chapter Seven: 1971 - 1979 65

Chapter Eight: 1980 - 1999 70

Chapter Nine: 2000 onwards 91

References

Reference: Initial First Match of the Tour 98

Final Summary 100

Final Notes 122

ACKNOWLEDGEMENTS

In compiling this book, I have had to draw on many records to collate the factual information as recorded.

I would thank Cricket Archive for their extensive detailed material, scorecards, and player profiles, and as regards the photographs I have introduced I would thank Worcester News, for their permission to use their photographs and my thanks to both Worcester People and Places and Bill Gwilliam for the permission to use their photographs.

Tim Jones has guided me and provided me with some photographs, and I would also thank Chris Wynne-Davies for detailed information and photograph concerning the Coventry Family.

Every attempt has been taken to seek permission for copyright material used in this book. However, if inadvertently copyright material has been introduced without permission or acknowledgement I apologise and will make the necessary correction at the earliest opportunity.

Similarly, every care has been taken to gather the detailed information, but it is acknowledged by the author that there is a likelihood over so many years that items may not have been recorded correctly. Again, if any come to light correction will be made to ensure that the factual information is there for future generations.

I would wish to thank Debbie Taylor for her technical expertise in helping edit and process the information in this book, and to Orphans Press of Leominster for the final production of "The First Square".

I have throughout the creation of this book confirmed that St Richard's Hospice Worcester will benefit from sales achieved, and I will take this opportunity to thank various people who have helped this book happen.

My great friend John Elliott who in the 1990's encouraged me to stand for election to the committee at the club, and who subsequently as chairman asked me to be his vice chairman for four years. To the committee members and club officials I served with during my time on the committee whose company I greatly enjoyed both in meetings but also on match days, and also to sitting and listening to former presidents of the club, who as Worcestershire cricketers had been my school boy heroes.

To the many players who I enjoyed watching who became good friends, and of course to my late wife Linda who enjoyed so much of the social side of the club, especially the benefit events.

And finally to my friends who encouraged me over the last fifteen months to complete this book.

Jack Randall   2024

THE FIRST SQUARE – FOREWORD

BY TIM JONES
WORCESTERSHIRE CCC CLUB HISTORIAN

In 2014, Richard Bentley produced a wonderfully nostalgic book about New Road, called *A Special Place*. It is a profusely illustrated collection of cricketing extracts from many cricketers, writers and journalists, all of whom share their love for this unique venue of ours.

Jack Randall in *The First Square* has continued with this love affair we have with New Road and explores how seeing his first game against the touring Pakistan team in 1954 helped nurture his passion for the game …and the New Road ground.

This love of New Road was put sharply into focus by one of Worcestershire's brightest prospects whose involvement as a professional cricketer ended abruptly.

During World War I, the promising career of all-rounder Frank Chester was cut short when he lost his right arm fighting in Salonika. In his book *How's That*, he comments: *They said I'd be back in six months when I left Worcester to join the Army in August 1915. Not until May 1948 – nearly 33 years after – did I next set foot on the ground which I grew to love.*

In the face of adversity, Chester became the leading umpire of his generation but until regulations changed in 1948, was not eligible to stand in matches involving his former county, hence the 33-year hiatus.

When his chance finally came, he admitted to being deeply *moved* by the reception he received from the crowd and *the visit to Worcester tore at my heart strings, but it also uplifted me. The*

Cathedral chimes sounding over the green and pleasant scene helped to remind me of what a wonderful improver of human relations the game of cricket can be.

In this book, Jack Randall has captured what the 'green and pleasant scene' first looked like to the touring teams he first saw and who, for so many years, began their tour with the customary opening fixture against Worcestershire.

It's hard to imagine that players of the calibre of Don Bradman, Gary Sobers and the three W's (Clyde Walcott, Frank Worrell and Everton Weekes) all played their inaugural, first-class match in this country on the New Road square.

Woven into these stories are recollections of Jack's own experience of what these early season matches meant to him. They are complemented with personal anecdotes and match reports, plus brief statistical summaries of each game, all of which provide a unique insight into what life was like for those who appeared on *The First Square*.

CHAPTER ONE: MY BOYHOOD INTEREST IN CRICKET

I have named this book *The First Square*, it's about the cricket square at New Road, but it is not a book about the ground, I have left many angles for future cricket writers, and so much has been written already. I am not writing about floods, or any developments or structures since original acquisition, or the view, which we know is second to none, and world renowned or the composition of the soil.

But who knows, on 3 September 1651, one might picture Cavaliers heading out over our ground to meet the Roundhead Army of Oliver Cromwell on the battlefield on the fields nearer Powick, and probably hastily retreating to get back into the city over the bridge.

In 1786 did John Adams, and Thomas Jefferson, both future Presidents of America, ride out across our ground to view "the battlefield where democracy was born," according to John Adams. That was on 8 April 1786 so we were attracting tourists even then.

John Adams was the second President of America, 1797-1801 and Thomas Jefferson, the third 1801-1809.

The records show that Queen Elizabeth II, and Prince Philip visited the ground on 27 April 1957, and Elton John for a concert on 11 June 2006.

So, one day I was sitting in the Graeme Hick Pavilion in early 2023 near lunchtime, it was raining of course, and I was talking to Norman Gifford and the late Duncan Fearnley.

In conversation I mentioned that my very first visit to the county ground was when my mother brought me to the first day of the tourist match versus Pakistan in 1954.

I was nine, and of course it was the first day that Pakistan had played first class cricket in this country. I suddenly thought, why not write a book about those tourist matches.

Had any one before me just considered those annual initial, first class matches played on that square. This book concentrates ultimately on that one square. What a strange book to centre on one piece of grass, several battle grounds no doubt have been written about, and maybe to the combatants it could qualify as a battleground. New Road has witnessed many hard-fought matches since 1899.

Why that match, where had my interest in Cricket come from. My grandfather was undoubtedly a keen cricketer and played for the Worcestershire Farmers. From the old family photograph, it was highly likely that they played at New Road around 1900.

Thinking about it further and accepting that I was actually born approximately one quarter of a mile from the ground in Alexander Road, St Johns, I think we must look to 1953 when my father bought one of those new cabinets with a miniscule screen, for the village to sit round and watch the Coronation of our Queen Elizabeth II.

It was also the Ashes year with Lindsay Hassett's Australian tourists here to defend the Ashes which Australia had held since 1934.

I believe those Test matches were televised and I must have been glued to the little screen, and especially the Oval Test when England won the Ashes back after a span of 19 years.

CHAPTER ONE: MY BOYHOOD INTEREST IN CRICKET

That I am sure fired my imagination of the game of cricket, which was strengthened by my grandmother giving me Peter West's *Fight for the Ashes Book*, 1953, as my Christmas present. A wonderful record of every match on that tour starting with the usual friendly match at Arundel Castle, where the tourists played the Duke of Norfolk's X1, followed by the first tour match at New Road, Worcester.

Thinking about Alexander Road, I would probably have been three and in the garden when Sir Donald Bradman scored yet another century at New Road. I would be delighted to learn of a Worcestershire supporter reading this book who was actually on the ground that day to witness that innings. I know that those opening matches attracted TV, Radio, and the sporting Press, and huge crowds to see the tourists play. Some already superstars, some future great cricketers. The purpose of this book is to identify some of those who made their debut for their country in England on our riverside meadow, in the twentieth century, and there are many as this book will identify. It is for the reader to add their own memories and make further enquiry of their favourite cricketers. Cricket has moved so fast now, no longer the season long tourists visit. Now it's just jet in, and play Test cricket, and One Day Internationals and T20's.

Future generations of cricket followers will never understand the joy of a full summer tour. The importance to each County fixture list, and especially Worcester if it was the opening first class match.

So, in my garden on that Bradman day there may have been a huge roar as he reached his century. His fourth successive century, in his four visits to New Road. But would it have been a louder roar than when Tommy Skuse, 18 years old, scored for Worcester City in the 9th minute against Liverpool in the third round of the FA cup on 15th January 1959, when before a crowd of 15,111, at St George's Lane, Worcester City won 2 -1. They say even St Johns new Worcester had scored twice the sound carrying across the city. At least I can say I was there!! It was certainly Worcester City's finest hour, or to be more precise, an hour and a half.

That in itself begged a question, I wondered what the largest attendance at a sporting occasion in Worcester was. Although I will write more about one of the great families of Worcestershire who were both instrumental in the formation of the county club and were involved with the club in one form or another until 2002.

I found that the Coventry family were very involved in the staging of what I believe was the largest sporting occasion in Worcester.

I believe it was on January 7, 1824 on Pitchcroft when Tom Spring, the English Prize fighting champion, was matched against Paddy Langan, the Irish champion.

Reports suggest that a crowd of 40,000 attended, and during the fight two stands collapsed, with unfortunately one person dying, and a number of supporters injured.

Tom Spring had stayed the previous night at Croome Court as the guest of Lord Coventry, and the Lord's son, the Viscount Deerhurst was timekeeper for the fight, which commenced at 1.40pm and finally ended in the 77th Round at 4.15pm with Tom Spring the winner. Various reports suggest it might have been 84 rounds, but as rounds were invariably of different length the correct count might be fairly irrelevant.

CHAPTER ONE: MY BOYHOOD INTEREST IN CRICKET

The fight was for a purse of 300 gold sovereigns.

So, I must return to the theme of this book, as those tourist matches contain amazing facts about world cricketers and their first match at first class level at Worcester.

Not every tour started at Worcester, though I have included any tourist's first class fixture each season when that was not the case for consistency. One or two were I felt too important to omit.

It was 1929 when Worcestershire hosted the first, first class match of the tour, but the next chapter will look briefly at cricket in Worcestershire in the nineteenth century and outline its growth throughout the county.

I will however take this opportunity to mention the 1955 opening tourist match against South Africa. The weather was somewhat cold, many sweaters were worn, and a Worcestershire victory was achieved with Martin Horton enjoying a very good match.

I spent the three days huddled up in the old cowshed as it was referred to, with my Uncle Les who taught me a great deal about cricket. The building was demolished the next year and the Ladies Pavilion constructed on the site.

But he always disappeared at about 4.30pm, and there was suddenly a lot of noise and laughter in the Public Bar on the other side of the ground. He was a great entertainer, and no doubt was giving his personal account of the days play to everyone present.

Uncle Les loved his cricket but was prone to entertainment and acting. Either in the bar at the cricket or once, when my Auntie Moll was furious with him at Cheltenham Races when he disappeared and she found him on the concourse with his raincoat folded in front of him, doing a Prince Monolulu impression selling racing tips. I think the call was "I gotta horse"

And again, I would like to mention 1956 and another visit by Australia, as by then I had an autograph book and was out to get autographs.

How lucky I was that a very big Australian walked by returning from the nets, and he sat down and talked to me about cricket. It seemed like half an hour but was probably about five minutes. I was in the presence of the great Keith Miller. What an autograph I still have. Still acknowledged as the greatest Australian all-rounder.

If only I had known of his war time record as a fighter pilot. I will leave it to the reader to find his remark about stress in cricket in a Michael Parkinson interview. I will mention more of his career later.

These matches will be detailed later in the chapters, but again 1957 brought a West Indian team so full of talent, famous names Walcott, Weekes and Worrell, Ramadhin and Valentine of calypso fame but also the future of West Indies cricket in Gary Sobers and Wes Hall, Roy Gilchrist and Rohan Kanhai.

CHAPTER TWO: EARLY CRICKET IN THE COUNTY

I felt I wanted to spend a little time exploring the early days of cricket in Worcestershire in the nineteenth century and in fact it leads to the acquisition of New Road before the turn of the century. I am sure it would have started in the eighteenth century, but I will leave that history to others to research about Worcestershire cricket.

Again, I leave the detail to better writers than I, but it becomes apparent that several of our stately homes in Worcestershire developed their own Cricket Grounds, no doubt for their own enjoyment and the opportunity to develop their house parties during the summer with invited teams. But no doubt to keep the ground in good state and also to reward the local village community who worked on the estate, the birth of village cricket was created. I can think of Croome Court, Ombersley Court and Witley Court all having grounds within their parks, and especially the most documented at Hagley Hall, and I am sure there are others.

The Lyttelton family of Hagley Hall had their own ground, with Hagley Cricket Club being formed in 1834. By the 1860's matches are recorded against Lye, Kidderminster, Kinver, Bromsgrove, Dudley, Bewdley and Halesowen.

Chester Road North, the home of Kidderminster Cricket Club was opened in 1870, Himley Cricket Club in 1887, and even Martley CC claiming evidence of a team in 1859.

William Ward, 1st Earl of Dudley, the family originally living at Himley Hall had actually played first class cricket between 1838 and 1842 whilst at Oxford University. The family moved to Witley Court in 1837 and his generosity to Worcester Cathedral is well documented. He died in 1885 having been President of the MCC in 1864/1865.

The second Earl of Dudley was President of Worcestershire CCC in 1913 to 1914, and he had both a cricket ground and golf course at Witley Court.

Ombersley Cricket Club had been formed in 1863.

On the 28 and 29 August 1844 on Hartlebury Common, a Worcestershire Eleven played an Eleven representing Shropshire. Two things are apparent. Already a Cricket team is considered to be eleven players and also that the match featured two innings each side.

There are instances in this book where teams of different strength were matched against the better teams of the age.

From the scorecard Worcestershire appear to have batted first and were all out for 27.

Shropshire replied 61 all out. Worcestershire then replied with 55 all out, thus allowing Shropshire to win by nine wickets.

Sadly, no bowling statistics were recorded, but it is recorded as being a four ball per over match. Round arm bowling had been legalised in 1835, when the bowler was allowed to deliver the ball at shoulder height, and in 1864 the MCC rewrote the laws on bowling to allow the bowler to bring his arm through at any height providing he kept it straight and did not throw the ball.

A second Hartlebury Common match is recorded as a one-day match on 6 August 1846. A Worcestershire team

CHAPTER TWO: EARLY CRICKET IN THE COUNTY

playing Herefordshire again four balls per over, but this time Worcestershire scored 124 in their first innings, with Herefordshire replying with a total innings of 19. Following on Herefordshire did no better amassing 20.

A Worcestershire win by an innings and 85 runs. The language of cricket was in place.

Also, in 1846 there is recorded a Worcestershire XXII playing William Clarke's All- England XI at Powick Ham.

There are references to matches being played in Worcester on a ground behind the Talbot Inn in the Tything. Would this be what we know as Flagge Meadow. There is reference to cricket being played there in 1886. The Worcester Canal had been completed in 1815, which provides one boundary to Flagge Meadow and St Oswald's playing fields.

Matches on Pitchcroft are mentioned before the unofficial Worcestershire team moved to the Pleasure Gardens, later referred to as Boughton Park.

1864 had seen the first recorded unofficial county championship winner as Surrey, and 1865 Nottinghamshire.

In England, were we concerned that Abraham Lincoln had been assassinated in 1865 or that General Robert E Lee had surrendered the Confederate Army of North Virginia to signal the end of the American Civil War. Not after it had been become legal to bowl overarm in 1864.

George William, 9th Earl of Coventry (1838-1930), was another important person in Worcestershire Cricket. He became a member of the Marylebone Cricket Club in 1856 at the age of 18 and played for the I Zingari Club at Lords against the Household Brigade. He attended the inaugural meeting on 4th March 1865 at the Star Hotel, when Worcestershire County Cricket Club was formed and served on the first committee. He had previously become the President of the Marylebone Cricket Club in 1859, the then youngest President since 1825 and remained the youngest President until 2021. He was president of the County Cricket club from 1877 to 1907, again in 1920, and also from 1925 to 1930.

His son, then Viscount Deerhurst was President from 1921-1923.

One other son, Henry played at Eton and played for the Marylebone Cricket Club.

Another son Charles also played for the MCC and both sons played for Worcestershire at times.

Another interesting match is recorded on 18 August 1876, when Worcestershire played Lord Coventry's XI at Croome Park, High Green. 30 years later than the 1846 match previously mentioned but still four balls an over.

Worcestershire scored 122, with Lord Coventry's team responding with 68 all out.

The Lord scored 13, and sadly extras were the highest scorer with 19.

Worcestershire played a second innings scoring 81 all out and that appears to be the end of the match with Worcestershire recorded as winning on the first innings.

I found a scorecard of a match at Boughton Park on 2 and 3 August 1886, when both Coventry brothers played for the MCC against Worcestershire.

A four ball over match shown as match drawn, where Henry scored 1, and Charles 6, in the first innings and Henry scored 6 in the second innings and Charles 0.

CHAPTER TWO: EARLY CRICKET IN THE COUNTY

Charles toured South Africa in 1889 on R G Warton's tour. He played throughout the tour and two matches were designated as Test matchcs, he played the first at Port Elizabeth where he scored 12, the second at Newlands, Cape Town, where he scored 1 not out.

He was obviously a military man and had spent much of the 1890's in South Africa. He is linked to serving in Rhodesia during the 1893 Matabele uprising and also the ill-fated Jameson Raid on the South African Republic, the Transvaal in 1895/1896, for which he received a jail sentence.

The first recorded match where Worcestershire played as Worcestershire County Cricket Club after its inauguration, took place at Bromsgrove School on 29 April 1865.

Having detailed the Coventry family in Worcestershire's cricketing history, I must detail the other Worcestershire family with deep connections, the Lyttelton family of Hagley Hall.

Lord George Lyttelton, the 4th Baron, had actually played cricket whilst at Cambridge University, and importantly chaired that inaugural meeting at the Star Hotel on the 4 March1865. He became the first president of the county club, being president from 1865 until 1876. At Cambridge he was recorded as a right-hand batsman and underarm bowler.

The Lyttelton family provided four presidents of the MCC, Alfred Lyttelton, Charles Lyttelton the 8th Viscount Cobham, John Lyttelton the 9th Viscount Cobham, and Charles Lyttelton the 10th Viscount Cobham.

Charles, the 10th Viscount played 104 first class matches for Worcestershire between 1932 and 1939, captaining the side 1936-1939.

THE FIRST SQUARE

The 9th Viscount Cobham was President of Worcestershire in 1924 and 1936-1949. C G Lyttleton, his father was President 1908-1910 and 1915-1919.

During his career he scored 3,181 runs, with one century, and took 32 wickets.

Again, before we move forward too quickly, we must look at the link between Worcestershire and Dr W G Grace.

The earliest record I can find of W G Grace playing in Worcestershire is a match at Boughton Park on 27 and 28 June 1870. This was actually a Worcestershire 22 playing a United North of England Eleven with W G Grace playing for Worcestershire. Can you believe a scorecard reading Worcestershire won by 14 wickets!!

The North of England batted first with W G Grace opening the bowling. Not impressive bowling statistics: 16 overs, 7 maidens, 1 wicket for 36, with one wide!

They totalled 127, and the 22 of Worcestershire replied with 113, of which W G Grace opening the batting contributed 74.

G Howitt who opened the bowling for the North recorded 35.1 overs, 16 maidens, 11 wickets for 48 runs.

The North were then bowled out for 87 with W G taking 2 for 12, and Worcestershire scored the necessary runs losing 7 wickets and the Dr scoring 38.

On the 29 June again at Boughton Park he captained his own 12, against R Iddison's 13.

The match was decided on first innings with R Iddison's the winners. The Doctor had scored 46.

Two interesting matches in 1871. One at Boughton Park on the 3, 4 and 5 August when a Worcestershire 22 played a united

CHAPTER TWO: EARLY CRICKET IN THE COUNTY

South of England eleven. Worcestershire were captained by H Foster, of whose family much will be written later, and the Earl of Coventry also played for Worcestershire in that match.

In a first innings of 132 unfortunately both gentlemen are recorded as failing to score.

Worcestershire lost the match, but H Foster scored 57 in his second innings whilst unfortunately the Earl succeeded in recording a pair.

The second match of no significance to Worcestershire was actually an appearance of W G Grace playing for the United South of England Eleven against Birmingham played on Aston Lower Fields, Trinity Road, Birmingham, on 11, 12 and 13 September 1871. What a development there in the next decade.

There are two matches I would like to mention out of sequence, both matches actually played at New Road. The first, a non-first class match between Worcestershire and London County on 29, 30, and 31 May 1899.

The reason I introduce this match was because W G Grace was playing for London County, and in a drawn match he scored 175 not out in their second innings. The second match was on 14 and 15 May 1900, again against London County.

Worcestershire were captained by H K Foster, and London County opener was again W G Grace. 30 years after his first appearance at Boughton Park. He was aged 21 when he first played at Boughton Park, 50 when he played at New Road.

He managed 30 in the first innings and 20 in the second, with London County victorious in the match.

This was now a six ball over match and W G Grace opened the bowling taking 4 wickets in the first innings and 5 for 66 in the second.

I now very much leave the history of Worcestershire Cricket in the second half of the nineteenth century to other writers save to say Worcestershire did play matches all over the County though Boughton Park was the centre.

One interesting match was Lord Dudley's 18 playing the Australians on their inaugural tour of the British Isles in 1878. The match was played fittingly at Tipton Road, Dudley.

England and Australia had designated themselves as Test Playing countries in 1877, followed by South Africa in 1889. The West Indies joined the elite in 1928 New Zealand in 1930 and India in 1932.

Pakistan joined in 1952, Sri Lanka in 1982, Zimbabwe in 1992, Bangladesh in 2000 and Ireland in 2018.

I should now write about Paul Foley, because he became the influencer (a modern term) for our Cricketing County.

Born of a Stourbridge Ironmaster family in 1857, educated at Eton, and Christ Church, Oxford, becoming a barrister in 1880.

He had however become a member of the Marylebone Cricket Club in 1878. He actually played one match for them against Somerset in 1891, but he had similarly become associated with Worcestershire in 1878.

In 1885 he became co- secretary of the club a position he held until 1887, and then became Honorary Secretary in 1892. Through his Cricketing connections and his undoubted ability as an Administrator he helped create the Minor Counties Championship in 1895, with Worcestershire joining the inaugural Minor Counties Championship that year.

The team moved from one day amateurs to three-day professionals and having shared the title as Champions in 1895, Worcestershire went on to win the Minor Counties

CHAPTER TWO: EARLY CRICKET IN THE COUNTY

Championship in 1896, 1897, and 1898. This allowed the application to succeed for Worcestershire to join the First-Class County Championship in 1899.

It is interesting to note that in 1895 our Minor County home Matches were played at the War Memorial Ground, Amblecote Stourbridge, Malvern College, Tipton Road, Dudley, Chester Road North, Kidderminster, and on 19 August 1895 at Boughton Park.

Those matches were all five ball overs. So many years before we were introduced to the new Hundred Competition with its five ball overs or sets.

Paul Foley as Honorary Secretary had during that year started negotiations to acquire the lease of fields on New Road, from the Dean and Chapter of Worcester Cathedral.

The acquisition was achieved in 1896, and Paul Foley is reported as personally paying for the pavilion to be built.

The first Minor County Match recorded as played at New Road was against Berkshire on the 28 and 29 July 1897, Worcestershire captained by H K Foster won the match by an innings and 24 runs. This game was played with five ball overs and the result gave Worcestershire one point, and Berkshire minus one point!

Worcestershire's top score was E G Arnold with 53, H K Foster scored 26, and his brother R E Foster 26.

So, 1897 Worcestershire have played their first Minor County Match at New Road.

We can now move to the next Chapter where we take Worcestershire through first class matches, and I can look at our matches against touring sides until 1929 when I can really start to develop the purpose of this book.

CHAPTER THREE:
THE FIRST-CLASS COUNTY

Worcestershire Farmers Cricket Team. Circa 1897/1900.

*W L & R E Foster. Worcs V Essex, July 1899, when they each scored centuries in each innings.
By Courtesy of Bill Gwilliam and Worcester People and Places.*

CHAPTER THREE: THE FIRST-CLASS COUNTY

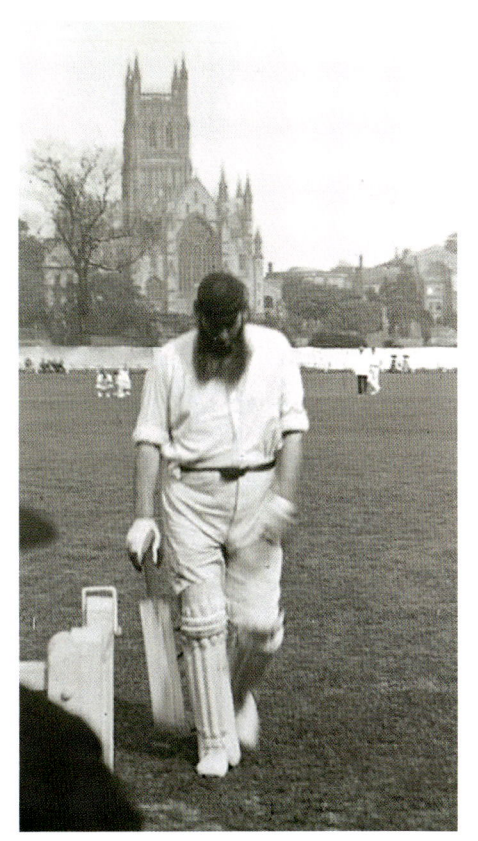

Dr W G GRACE. By Courtesy of Bill Gwilliam and Worcester People and Places.

July 1928 - H H I H Gibbons and W V Fox. Worcs v West Indies

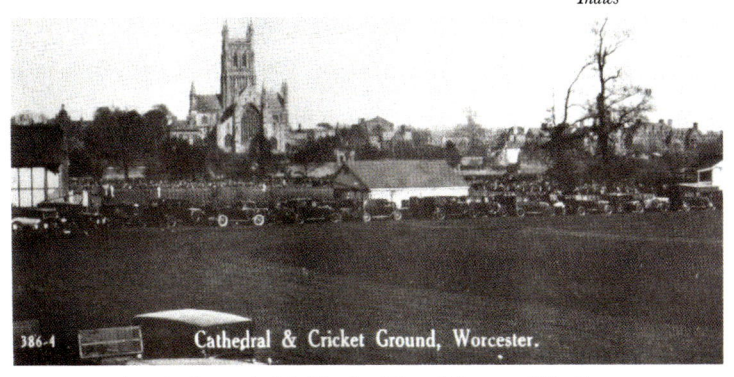

An early photograph of the New Road Ground. Courtesy of Tim Jones.

As I have said, my aim in this book is to look at the opening first class tourist matches and there are a lot of them, but again, I felt I had to let Worcestershire develop in the period to 1929, before we look at the opening first class tour matches at New Road.

Sadly between 1899 and 1929 years were lost because of the First World War and sadly many young aspiring cricketers as well. But in a large part of that period, we have the Fostershire years.

Mention was made of H Foster playing for Worcestershire in 1871, but we now enter the era of his sons.

I think I should immediately mention the county match versus Hampshire in July 1899 when W L Foster scored 140 and R E Foster 134 in the first innings, a stand of 161, and in the second innings W L Foster scored 172 not out and R E Foster 101 not out, an unbroken stand of 219 runs.

As to Tour matches in that period in 1900 at New Road, on 14, 15, and 16 June Worcestershire played a visiting team from the West Indies. This was deemed not to be a first-class match but Worcester were victorious by 215 runs.

In our first innings we scored 307, with H K Foster scoring 79, the West Indies replying with 187. I note that L S Constantine scored 8 in that first innings.

Worcestershire scored 257 for 9 declared in their second innings and then dismissed the visitors for 162. Again, L S Constantine only contributed 12. I mention L S Constantine because he was the father of L N (Sir Learie) Constantine, a great pre second world war West Indian cricketer who will be mentioned later in this chapter.

In 1901, Worcestershire entertained a touring side from South Africa on 15 ,16 and 17 July.

CHAPTER THREE: THE FIRST-CLASS COUNTY

This was deemed a first-class match, and amazingly ended as a tie.

Worcestershire were captained by R E Foster, and South Africa won the toss and chose to bat scoring 293.

By the close of play on day one, Worcestershire were 121 for 6.

Their innings closed on day two on 224. The tourists were then bowled out for 140, leaving Worcester to score 210 to win. By close of play on day two Worcestershire were 84 for 5, so they did well to recover to score all but one run to win the match.

On 10, 11 and 12 July 1902, Worcestershire entertained Australia. An Australian Team, full of great cricketing names. C Hill, M A Noble, S E Gregory, W W Armstrong with their captain J Darling.

This is a well-documented Australian Tour, five Test Matches were played, with Australia winning the series two / one with two tests drawn. This was the fourth consecutive Ashes series that Australia retained the unique Trophy, and in fact only lost two of their 39 matches on the tour.

An interesting unrelated fact was that the second test match was played at Bramall Lane, Sheffield, the only Test Match ever staged there. Australia won that match by 143 runs.

Returning to the Worcestershire fixture, one could say Worcestershire were lucky that Victor Trumper was rested for the match. He set many batting records on that tour, and whilst it was recorded as a very wet summer, he amassed 2,570 runs in 53 innings.

On the first morning of the Old Trafford Test that tour he scored 103 before lunch.

So, at Worcester the Australians won the toss on the morning of 10 July and decided to bat.

They were bowled out by the close of play for 274 runs. R A Duff, the Australian opener, top scoring with 90, C Hill 29, and M A Noble 56.

A Bird of Worcestershire had taken 6 wickets for 69 runs off 18 overs.

Worcestershire commenced day two on 5 for 1, and eventually scored 202. By the close of play Australia were 169 for 5, and reached 199 all out, on day three.

Worcestershire could not mount a serious attempt at winning the match and were bowled out for 97.

It should be noted that in the Worcestershire team were both H K Foster as captain and R E Foster.

The tourists in 1903 are a quiz question for sure. Would you believe the Gentlemen of Philadelphia.

They played at New Road, on 13, 14 and 15 July.

Worcestershire captained by H K Foster, won by 215 runs having scored 388 in their first innings and 205 in their second.

Philadelphia replied with 233 and 145.

1904 saw a return of a South African Touring side, captained by F Mitchell. They played at New Road, on the 2 ,3 and 4 July.

H K Foster won the toss and decided to bat, he opened the batting with F L Bowley and whilst Bowley was out for 0, HK went on to score 107. Worcestershire scored 227,

South Africa replied with 161. E G Arnold taking 5 for 59. Worcestershire added 259 in their second innings with H K Foster now batting at number four making 53, and E G Arnold at five making 85.

CHAPTER THREE: THE FIRST-CLASS COUNTY

Worcestershire sealed a good victory bowling South Africa out for 188 in their second innings with Arnold taking another three wickets and R D Burrows 5 for 43.

1905 saw a return of an Australian touring side. The match played at New Road on the 3, 4, and 5 August saw Australia win the toss and score 330 in their first innings. There had been no play on day one but this time Worcestershire did see Victor Trumper score 110 on that second day with M A Noble scoring 113 and W W Armstrong 55.

Worcestershire replied with 78 all out. A match with four Fosters in the team. W L, R E, G N, and HK. R E had top scored with 31.

Following on Worcestershire were 51 for five at the close.

The Australians actually lost the test series on that tour.

There were no visiting tourists to New Road in 1906 and 1907, though 1906 had seen a West Indies Tour and 1907 a South African team.

1908 saw a return of the Gentlemen of Philadelphia and this time they were victorious over the home team. Just for the record on 27 August 1908 one Donald Bradman was born in Australia.

Worcestershire may well have thought they were in the driving seat having bowled out the visitors for 138 with A Bird taking 6 for 50, and then scoring 192 in their first innings with H K Foster scoring 65, but the resolute team from Philadelphia scored 278 in their second innings with A M Wood their centurion on 132.

Worcestershire were bowled out for 129 and the gentlemen won by 95 runs.

1909 saw another Tour by the Australians. A successful tour for them winning the Test Series two / one.

Worcestershire were comprehensively beaten on the 8, 9, and 10 July.

Australia, captained by M A Noble, won the toss, and chose to bat. By close of play on day one, they were 312 for six. V S Ransford had scored 138 when Australia were finally bowled out for 389. The Australian team had such names as W Bardsley, V T Trumper, S E Gregory, W W Armstrong and M A Noble.

By the close of play on day two Worcestershire were 73 for two, in their second innings having been bowled out for 151 in their first innings.

Although represented by both H K and W L Foster Worcestershire scored 126 in their second innings and were thus defeated by an innings and 112 runs.

W W Armstrong took nine wickets in the match.

There appears to have been no international tour in 1910, and in 1911 England welcomed an Indian team, under the 19 year-old Maharaja of Patiala Bhupinder Singh.

It was reported as a disappointing tour winning only two of twenty-three matches and I have no record of them playing Worcestershire on that tour.

The tour is well documented as the Maharaja spent time with King George V and attended Royal Ascot with the King. His wonderful outfits captured the fashion press at the time.

It is reported that he travelled separately from the team on the tour on a deluxe train whilst the rest of the team travelled more modestly.

In July however he contracted tonsilitis resulting in further complications and he returned to India prematurely taking his aide with him who was the Tourists best batsman.

CHAPTER THREE: THE FIRST-CLASS COUNTY

1912 saw both Australia and South Africa visiting the UK to play in a triangular tournament and Worcestershire played both.

The South African team came to Worcester on 23, 24 and 25 May, and whilst there was no play on day one, they won the toss and asked Worcester to bat.

Worcester were bowled out for 50. There was not a Foster in the team.

South Africa replied with 298, and whilst Worcestershire scored 206 in their second innings, the match was lost by an innings and 42 runs.

In August on the 12, 13 and 14, Worcestershire played the visiting Australians, but the match was played at Tipton Road, Dudley.

Again, Worcestershire batted first but were bowled out for 143. This match we had three Fosters playing. H K, G N, and R E. G N had scored 62 not out, and R E 26. H K had failed to score.

The Australians replied with a large total of 407, very much thanks to W Bardsley scoring 176 not out. There was no play on day three and so the match was drawn. This the record books tell me was R E Foster's last appearance in first class cricket.

In the many records of the Fosters playing for Worcestershire, all 7 of the sons of the Rev'd Henry Foster and his wife Sophia, played for Worcestershire. One of their four daughters, Cicily, played Golf for England. One of the other daughters married W Greenstock who also played 7 first class matches for the county.

Books far better than this have been dedicated to the Fosters and I merely mention that H K Foster captained

Worcestershire in 1899, and 1900. And then 1902 to 1910 and also 1913.

R E 'Tip' Foster captained the team in 1901 but business interests curtailed his cricketing career, despite batting records being set everywhere, and also captaining England at Football in 1902 against Wales. He was awarded the captaincy of England for the tour of Australia in 1903/1904 and set a long unbroken record of scoring 287 in his debut innings in Test Cricket at the Sydney Cricket ground.

He is the only man who has captained England at both Football and Cricket.

M K Foster captained Worcestershire 1923/1925.

We then had a long period of no international visitors to this country, with the First World War being the cause.

In fact, in 1919, an Australian Imperial forces team started the rebuilding of International Cricket and they played at New Road on 18 and 19 July.

Worcestershire batted first on winning the toss but were quickly dismissed for 120. J M Gregory taking 7 wickets for 56 runs. The Imperial Forces replied with a commanding 450 for 4 declared. C E Pellew 195 not out and C B Willis 129 not out putting on an unbroken fifth wicket stand of 300.

H K Foster was playing in that match, but Worcester's second innings put up little resistance and they were bowled out for 127. Gregory again taking four wickets.

It is a recorded fact that Worcestershire could not compete in the championship that year, and 1920 had some disastrous results.

There was no touring party in 1920 and whilst a full Australian tour took place in 1921, they did not play a fixture at Worcester. Australia won that test series comfortably.

CHAPTER THREE: THE FIRST-CLASS COUNTY

Again in 1922 there was a small tour by Canada with no fixture against Worcester.

In 1923 the county was visited by the touring West Indians. Worcestershire now captained by M K Foster chose to bat and scored 223 on the second day, no play being possible on the first the 29 August. The West Indies replied with 145 all out.

Worcestershire's second innings ended on 175 for 9 wickets.

It is noted that L N Constantine played in that match. One of the most influential of early West Indian cricketers but also Worcestershire had a new bowler by the name of C F Root.

30 August and 1 September 1924 saw the visiting South African team, including A W Nourse, play at New Road. South Africa had asked Worcestershire to bat and duly bowled us out for 87. The reply was a well-constructed 276 with A W Nourse scoring 90. C F Root had taken 5 wickets though.

Worcestershire's second innings was little better totalling 161, so South Africa won by an innings and 28 runs.

No tour in 1925, but a very strong Australian team arrived for a two-day match on 7 and 8 July 1926. What names arrived. W Bardsley, A J Richardson, W H Ponsford, J M Gregory, W A S Oldfield and C V Grimmett.

Worcestershire under the captaincy of M K Foster, now had the high-class bowling of C F Fred Root. Australia batted first and scored 197. Root taking 4 for 61.

Worcestershire sadly replied with 120. Macartney taking 5 for 38 and Grimmett 4 wickets for two runs. What bowling figures 5 overs 3 maidens 4 wickets for 2 runs.

Australia scored 182 for 4 declared in their second innings Bardsley and Richardson both hitting half centuries, and

Worcestershire set 260 to win were then dismissed for 83. Grimmett taking a further 4 wickets.

Fred Root had joined Worcestershire from Derbyshire in 1921. He played in three Test Matches for England in 1926, taking 8 wickets. In his first-class career spanning 1910-1933 he took 1,512 wickets.

1927 saw Worcestershire play a first-class fixture against a visiting team from New Zealand. Played at New Road on 8, 9 and 10 June, New Zealand batted first and scored 276. There captain T C Lowry scored 74 and C C R Dacre 82.

Worcestershire replied with 222, but then in their second innings New Zealand scored 349 for 5 wickets declared. Two centurions, M L Page 140 not out and T C Lowry 106.

Worcestershire found it hard to chase down the 404 required and were bowled out for 209. Strangely the Worcestershire batsman W V Cox top scored in both innings with a score of 79. How does one research whether that has ever been achieved with a higher equal score.

So, this chapter ends in 1928, with a visit by the touring West Indies. A two-day match on 18 and 19 July.

West Indies won the toss and decided to bat reaching 410 for 6 wickets, a total they declared at overnight. E L G Hoad had scored 149.

Worcestershire on day two batted magnificently, with HHIH Gibbons scoring 200 not out, M Nichol 104, and W V Fox 104 not out. 439 for two at the close. And scored off 122 overs

So this chapter has brought the book to the point where I want to emphasise the importance of our square at New Road, in its role of introducing many international cricketers to their first, first-class match in England where they represented their Country. Already by 1928 many famous names have played at New Road, in County Matches and how I would like to research the visits of Jack Hobbs and others and some of our own Worcestershire players already mentioned but I know there are volumes on them already and it's not in the theme of this book.

It is interesting to find a little about W V Fox however. Born in Middlesbrough he was a right-hand Batsman and played for Worcestershire from 1923 to 1932. He also played Football for Middlesbrough, Wolverhampton Wanderers, Newport County and Exeter.

He played 163 first class matches scoring 6,654 runs and 11 centuries.

CHAPTER FOUR:
1929 - 1939

The Worcestershire Team of 1932. Captain C F Walters, with the Nawab of Pataudi, seated on his far left as we look at the photo. Courtesy of Worcester News

1924 the 9th Earl of Coventry, as President with the Worcestershire Team. By courtesy of the historian of the Coventry Family and Croome Court.

CHAPTER FOUR: 1929-1939

1929 brings me to the season where my book really starts, when the tourist party plays it's opening first class game at Worcester. There are seasons where this did not happen and I have attempted to stay to the theme of the first match of a tour, though I will cover various matches where the tour did not start at Worcester, as there are one or two which require mentioning.

1929 saw the South African tourists open their first-class tour at New Road on 1 May.

A three-day match with South Africa winning the toss and deciding to bat.

By close of play on day one, South Africa had reached 337 for 5. H W Taylor the opening batsman had scored 103 and H B Cameron, the captain was 87 not out, on his way to 102 the next morning.

South Africa declared at 444 for 8 wickets.

Worcestershire under M F S Jewell replied with 251 for 6 by the close of play on day two, with M F S Jewell scoring 68 and W V Fox 88.

On the third morning they were bowled out for 284 and were invited to follow on.

N A Quinn the South African bowler ended with impressive figures of 6 for 75 off 44 overs.

Worcestershire reached 262 for 7 wickets on day three, with W V Fox again contributing with 58, L Wright 50, and C V Tarbox 50 not out. The game thus ending as a draw.

Eight of the South African team made their debut in England in first class matches, including, H B Cameron, C L Vincent and B Mitchell.

That tour, South Africa played five tests but lost two and the other three were drawn.

1930 saw the Australians visit Worcester on the 30 April, for a three-day match. There was a Civic reception held at the Guildhall, but the Captain of Worcestershire, the Hon John Coventry, who was also Mayor that year, was ill and he missed both the dinner and the match. Cyril Walters the club secretary assuming the captaincy.

Again, the opening first class game of their tour, and we must immediately look at the Australian debutants. Eight in total, led by D G Bradman, but also V Y Richardson, E L á Beckett, A Jackson, A G Fairfax, P M Hornibrook, T W Wall and S J McCabe.

Worcestershire won the toss and decided to bat. They were dismissed in the 57th over for 131. C V Grimmett taking 4 for 38, and A G Fairfax 4 for 36.

I note both Cyril Walters and Fred Root were stumped by W A S Oldfield in that first innings.

The Australians replied with 492 for 8 declared, W M Woodfull the Australian Captain and opener scoring 133 and as Worcestershire were going to get used to in following visits Don Bradman batting at number three, the scorecards reading caught Walters bowled Brook 236

As if to emphasise the record book Bradman's innings included 28 fours. No sixes, too risky a shot.

It is recorded that in his entire career he only hit six 6's in Test and First Class Cricket. He was also only once run out in test cricket.

But in delving deep into Don Bradman, I found a reference to him hitting a century in 18 minutes off 22 balls in three overs, in 1931. Playing for Blackheath against Lithgow in Australia in a non-first class match he did indeed hit a century

CHAPTER FOUR: 1929-1939

in three overs, because in Australia between 1918/1919 and 1978/79 they played eight ball overs. The hundred consisted of 10 sixes and 9 fours. He went on to score 256 that innings.

Back to 1930, Worcestershire in reply scored 196. Root and Walters contributing 48 and 44 respectively. C V Grimmett again leading the Australian bowling with 5 for 46.

The Australians won the test rubber that year, with two wins, one loss and two drawn.

(D G Bradman scoring 974 runs during the series. Innings of 131 at Trent Bridge, 254 at Lords, and 232 at the Oval.)

New Zealand toured England in 1931 but did not open their tour at Worcester.

The match played from 20 May ended in a draw, though H H I H Gibbons scored 118 in the first innings.

India visited New Road on 18, 20 and 21 June,1932. The Nawab of Pataudi played for Worcestershire scoring 83 in the first innings but the home side were beaten by three wickets. Cyril Walters captained Worcestershire.

A Glamorgan man by birth, he played for Glamorgan from 1923-1928, joining Worcestershire 1928-1935. He played eleven tests for England between 1933-1934, and in 18 innings scored 784 runs, with one century, 102, and seven 50's.

He captained Worcestershire from 1931 to 1935.

1933 saw the visiting tourists from the West Indies. The match played on 31 May, 1 and 2 June. An interesting match in which Worcestershire won by 1 wicket.

The West Indies had batted first scoring 239, with Worcestershire replying with 215.

H H I H Doc Gibbons scoring 61 and Dick Howorth making his first-class debut for the home side, 68. The Tourists posted 257 in their second innings and Worcestershire reached the necessary 284 with one wicket spare. Thanks totally to the Nawab of Pataudi, 162 not out supported by Gibbons 64.

In fact, Worcestershire were 144 for one but lost the next eight wickets at regular intervals, the last pair adding 18 to secure the win.

This match was M F S Jewell's last appearance in first class cricket.

Dick Howorth went on to play until 1951, playing in 372 first class matches including 5 test matches for England. Scoring 11,479 runs with four centuries to his name and taking 1,345 wickets including 19 wickets at test level. He was a left-hand bat and orthodox left arm spin bowler.

Doc Gibbons played 383 matches for Worcestershire between 1927 and 1946, scoring 21,087 runs, including 44 centuries and 110 fifties.

The Nawab of Pataudi played for Worcestershire between 1932 and 1938. He played three tests for England, 1932/1933 and 1934 scoring one century. He played three tests for India in 1946. Overall, he scored 8,745 runs in first-class cricket, including 29 centuries with a highest score of 238 not out.

1934 saw the Australian Tourists open their first-class tour at Worcester on 2 and 3 of May.

Worcestershire having won the toss elected to bat but were bowled out in 56.3 overs for 112. C V Grimmett who seemed to enjoy bowling on this square took 5 for 53.

The Australians in reply had reached 199 for 3 at the close of day one. Don Bradman was already 112 not out. On day two the Australians were finally all out for 504, with Bradman

CHAPTER FOUR: 1929-1939

reaching his second double century at New Road, scoring 206. Howorth actually bowled Bradman and had bowling figures of 4 for 135.

Worcestershire in their second innings were dismissed for 95. Again Grimmett taking 5 for 27 and W J O'Reilly, making his first class debut for Australia 4 for 25.

Australia winning by an innings and 297 runs in two days.

1935 saw the touring South Africans open their first-class itinerary at New Road on 1, 2 and 3 May. There was no play on day one, Worcestershire captained by Cyril Walters won the toss and chose to bat. Unfortunately, they were bowled out for 90 in 27 overs.

R J Crisp making his first-class debut for South Africa taking 6 wickets for 34 runs in 9 overs.

At close of play on day two South Africa had just been bowled out for 351, with A D Nourse making his debut scoring 74, with the more experienced H B Cameron, the Captain of South Africa making 68 and E L Dalton 91.

On day 3 Worcestershire did little better than the first innings being bowled out for 95 in 40 overs.

R J Crisp taking 2 for 13, and A J Bell 5 for 22, having also taken 3 wickets for 6 runs in the first innings.

Five Test Matches were played that summer with South Africa winning the series 1-0, four being drawn.

1936 brought the Indian Tourists to Worcester, on 2, 4 and 5 May. The Indians were captained by the Maharamajkumar of Vizianagarm. His nickname was Vizzy, and he was one of the most controversial cricketers to have played for India.

I do not feel I should copy some of the stories during that tour, but the tour is recorded as not being a great success for Indian cricket although Vizzy was knighted while on the tour. And of course, made his first-class debut in England at New Road.

The actual match resulted in a Worcestershire win. Captained by C J Lyttleton he won the toss and asked India to bat. Worcestershire bowled out India on day one for 229, with Reg Perks taking 4 for 51, and S H Martin 4 for 42.

Worcestershire replied with 248, Dick Howorth top scoring with 58, and by close of play on day two, India were 130 for 9.

They were finally all out for 150, again with Reg Perks taking 5 for 37.

Worcestershire reached the target scoring 134 for 7 wickets. R H C Human scoring 68 not out.

It is noted that V M Merchant, made his debut for India in England.

At this time I should add that C J Lyttelton (ultimately became the 10th Viscount Cobham in July 1949,) and then an illustrious career as Governor General of New Zealand from 1957 to 1962. Receiving the Knight of the Garter in 1964, a Privy Counsellor in 1967 and GCVO in 1972 for his services to the Royal Household (Knight Grand Cross of the Royal Victorian Order). He played for Worcestershire from 1932-1939, captaining the team 1936-1939.

New Zealand toured England in 1937 but did not open their first-class tour at Worcester.

The match played in June ended in a Worcestershire win, and it is noted that W A Hadlee, the father of R J, B G, and D R Hadlee scored 58 in the New Zealand first innings.

CHAPTER FOUR: 1929-1939

1938, was of course another visit to Worcester by D G Bradman, now captain of the touring Australians and his team. The match had debuts in England for J H W Fingleton, and A L Hassett, amongst others.

Played on the 30 April, 2 and 3 May in front of a record crowd at New Road, Worcestershire captained by CJ Lyttleton invited the Australians to field.

By close of play on 30 April 1938 Australia were 474 for 6, Don Bradman having been dismissed ct Martin bowled Howorth, 258, including 33 fours. His first hundred taking 165 minutes and his second a further 75 minutes.

Australia were finally bowled out for 541, and Worcestershire replied with 268.

L O Fleetwood Smith a slow left arm wrist spin bowler had bowling figures of 29 overs 8 maidens 8 wickets for 98 runs.

In their second innings the home side were bowled out for 196 runs and thus were defeated by an innings and 77 runs.

The Test series was drawn 1 win each, with two drawn and the Manchester Test abandoned without a ball being bowled.

1939 was an interesting season in England. The one and only season when 8 ball overs were played. The Touring side were from the West Indies, and the tour sadly shortened by the impending World War.

The West Indies opened their first-class tour at New Road on 6 and 8 May.

Worcestershire were put in by the West Indies and bowled out in 29.2 overs for 83 runs.

Worcestershire again captained by C J Lyttleton restricted the tourists to 142 with Reg Perks taking 6 wickets and Dick Howorth 3.

The home team in their second innings scored 291, with E Cooper scoring 92 and S H Martin 94 and were then able to bowl out the tourists in the final innings for 147. Perks taking 5 for 48 and Howorth 4 for 42.

L N Constantine topped scored for the West Indies in their second innings with 47.

It is noted that J B Stollmeyer made his debut in England.

I will end this chapter at this point.

CHAPTER FIVE:
THE 1940'S AND 1950'S

1943 Baseball at New Road. Photos courtesy of Worcester News and Tim Jones.

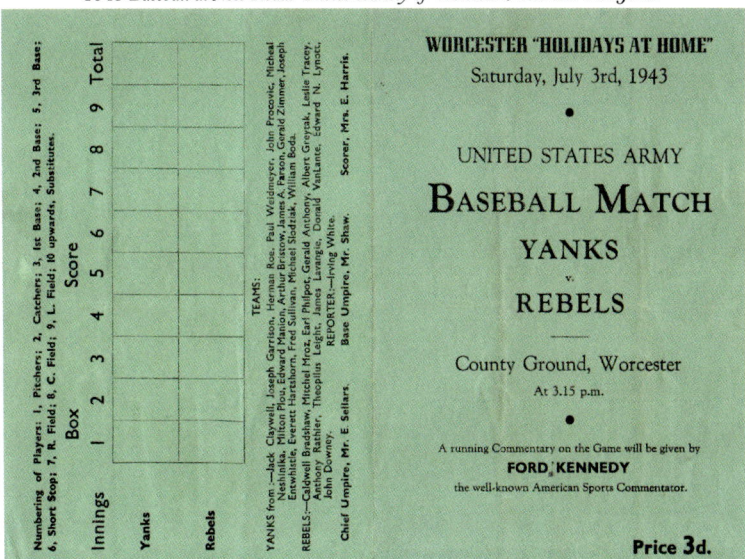

WORCESTER "HOLIDAYS AT HOME"
Saturday, July 3rd, 1943

•

UNITED STATES ARMY
BASEBALL MATCH
YANKS
v.
REBELS

County Ground, Worcester
At 3.15 p.m.

•

A running Commentary on the Game will be given by
FORD KENNEDY
the well-known American Sports Commentator.

Price **3d.**

Numbering of Players: 1, Pitchers; 2, Catchers; 3, 1st Base; 4, 2nd Base; 5, 3rd Base; 6, Short Stop; 7, R. Field; 8, C. Field; 9, L. Field; 10 upwards, Substitutes.

Innings	Box	1	2	3	4	5	6	7	8	9	Total
Yanks											
Rebels											

TEAMS:
YANKS from :—Jack Claywell, Joseph Garrison, Herman Roe, Paul Weidmeyer, John Procovic, Micheal Neslinkia, Milton Plos, Edward Manion, Arthur Bristow, James A. Parson, Gerald Zimmer, Joseph Entwhistle, Everett Hartshurn, Fred Sullivan, Michael Slodziak, William Boda.

REBELS—Aldwell Bradshaw, Mitchel Mroz, Earl Philpot, Gerald Anthony, Albert Greynak, Leslie Tracey, Anthony Rasher, Theoplius Leight, James Lavarge, Donald VanLante, Edward N. Lynott, John Downey.

REPORTER—Irving White.
Chief Umpire, Mr. E Sellars. Base Umpire, Mr. Shaw. Scorer, Mrs. E. Harris.

41

THE FIRST SQUARE

1948 Donald Bradman leading out the Invincibles. Courtesy of Worcester News.

1948 Official Welcome of the Australian Team at Shrub Hill. Alan White, the Worcestershire Captain greeting Donald Bradman. Courtesy of Worcester News.

CHAPTER FIVE: THE 1940'S AND 1950'S

1948 Australians led out to field before the media. Courtesy of Worcester News.

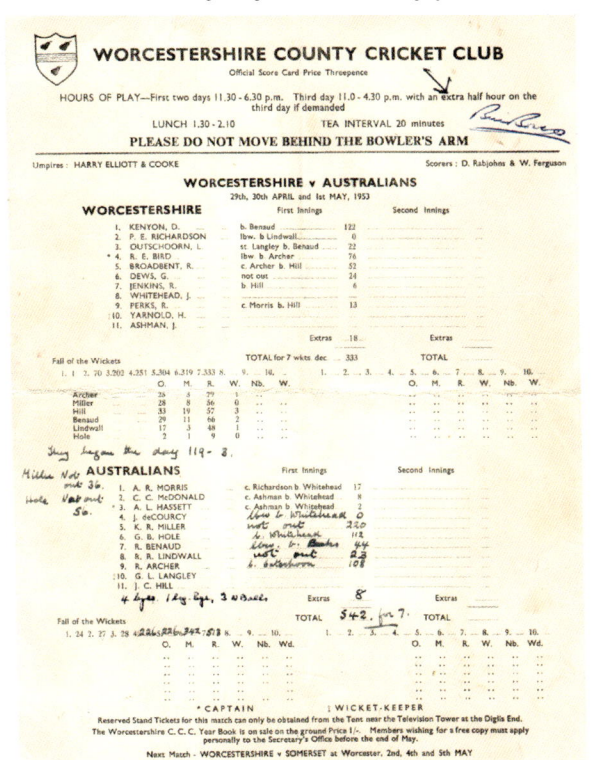

1953 Worcestershire V Australians Scorecard

THE FIRST SQUARE

WORCESTERSHIRE COUNTY CRICKET CLUB 1950
R.JENKINS L.OUTSCHOORN D.KENYON E.COOPER N.WHITING G.DEWS H.YARNOLD
P.JACKSON R.E.BIRD R.E.S.WYATT R.PERKS R.HOWORTH
(Captain)

1950 The Worcestershire Team of 1950. Courtesy of Tim Jones.

I will not dwell on the losses in the second World War. Many books have been written recording the Cricket still played in that period, both Forces Cricket and matches for Charity. I have introduced a couple of photographs showing Baseball being played at New Road during the War Years.

Mention must however be made of the Victory Tests played between May and August 1945, between a combined Australian Services XI, and an English National side.

The Matches were not given test match status but were classified as first-class matches. This answered my query as to when Keith Miller made his debut in this country.

The five matches ended as a drawn series, two wins each and one drawn.

England were captained by Wally Hammond, and the Australian Services by Lindsay Hassett, who had made his debut at Worcester in 1938.

CHAPTER FIVE: THE 1940'S AND 1950'S

Miller top scored for the Australian Services with 514 runs in the series. In fact, a century in the first innings of the first Test 105, and a further century of 118 in the fourth match.

It has been said he was one of the most charismatic, unpredictable and extrovert All Rounders that Cricket has ever seen.

He was awarded the MBE for his services to Cricket, and his portrait hangs in the Pavilion at Lords alongside Sir Donald Bradman and Victor Trumper, the only Australians to be so honoured.

So, in 1946 an Indian Touring party came to England and again commenced their first-class tour at Worcester.

Worcestershire under the captaincy of A P Singleton had been asked to bat on the 4 May and scored 191. Singleton top scoring with 47. India replied with 192, Perks taking 5 for 53.

The Worcestershire team were boasting players in Singleton, Howorth, Perks, Buller, Gibbons, Cooper, R O Jenkins, A F T White and P F Jackson playing for this post war county team with R E Bird and D M Young making their debuts for the county.

Worcestershire's second innings contained a century by Dick Howorth opening the batting, and the home team totalled 284.

The Indian team were bowled out for 267, with Worcestershire winning by 16 runs.

Another interesting fact emerging from this game was that India were captained by the Nawab of Pataudi who had played several seasons for Worcestershire before the War.

The South Africans toured England in 1947, again playing their opening first class match at Worcester on 30 April, 1 and 2 of May.

Allan White had taken the captaincy of the county, with Hugo Yarnold the wicket keeper. Worcester now saw Don Kenyon batting at three, and Bob Wyatt at four.

Having won the toss and deciding to bat the home team scored 202, with Ronald Bird top scoring with 79. A M B Rowan taking 5 for 59.

Worcestershire reduced South Africa to 167 all out with Reg Perks taking 5 for 66 and P F Jackson 4 for 63.

Worcestershire's second innings amounted to 111, with Rowan again taking 5 for 34, and N B F Mann 5 for 36.

The required runs were however difficult to get, and South Africa were bowled out for 107. Jackson taking 4 for 53 and Howorth 6 for 38. A home win by 39 runs.

Seven of the South Africans made their first-class debut, including J D Lindsay, N B F Mann, and A M B Rowan.

1948 saw the arrival of the Invincibles. The Australian Tourists led by Don Bradman.

The only team to play an entire tour of England without losing a match.

So much has been documented about this tour, it was known to be Bradman's last as he was 40 years old, record crowds attended match after match. Worcester was no exception with a record attendance of 32,000. Recorded as a slow pitch, cold and showery weather the match was played on 28, 29 and 30 April.

Allan White again captained the home team and having won the toss elected to bat.

CHAPTER FIVE: THE 1940'S AND 1950'S

Worcestershire were dismissed for 233, with C H Palmer scoring a resolute 85 in the face of a bowling attack of Lindwall, Miller, McCool, Toshack, and Johnson.

Don Kenyon had been lbw to Lindwall second ball.

By the close on day one, Australia were 10 for 0.

They batted throughout the second day reaching 377 for 6, and finally declared on 462 for 8 wickets.

As numerous books tell us Bradman recorded his fourth century in his four visits to Worcestershire and in his four innings at New Road.

But this time only 107. With 19 fours. The opener Arthur Morris scored 138, and Keith Miller ended with 50 not out.

Bradman had scored 236 in 1930, 206 in 1934, 258 in 1938 and now 107 in 1948. An average of 201.75 per innings.

Much can be, and has been written about his relationship with Keith Miller, Miller not responding well at times to Bradman's somewhat ruthless approach to cricket and to the discipline required in his team.

My mother told me that in 1948 there had been arranged a civic ball to welcome the Australian Team, but Bradman had asked his team not to attend as they were in England to play Cricket. To everyone's pleasure at 10.30pm Miller and Toshack walked in (it's what my mother told me!!!!).

Bradman's career ended having played 52 tests and scored 6,996 runs with 29 centuries. And in total in all first-class cricket 28,067 runs with 117 centuries. A top test innings of 334 and a first-class top score of 452 not out.

Well back to the match, Worcestershire in their second innings reached 212, only Laddie Outschoorn reached 50, and Australia won by an innings and 17 runs.

McCool taking 4 for 29 and Johnson 3 for 75.

First class debuts in England were achieved by I W G Johnson, R R Lindwall, C L McCool, D Tallon, E R H Toshack, and A R Morris.

Arthur Morris scored a century in his first innings in England. I will return to Sir Donald Bradman's average of 201.75 later.

1949. The New Zealand tourists did not open their tour in Worcester, but played on 7, 9 and 10 May.

The New Zealand team won comfortably, with centuries recorded by V J Scott and W M Wallace, and the captain W A Hadlee scoring 97 in their first innings of 425 all out. The home team replied with 279. New Zealand then added 220 for 5 declared, and Worcestershire were dismissed for 216, thus losing by 150 runs.

J R Reid, for New Zealand made his first-class debut in England. Bob Wyatt captained Worcestershire.

1950 saw a touring side from the West Indies. Captained by J C Goddard, and full of West Indies talent with A F Rae, and J B Stollmeyer, we saw the three W's.

F M M Worrell, E D Weekes, and C L Walcott, together with S Ramadhin, A Valentine, and Roy Marshall.

Weekes, Worrell and Walcott all played for Barbados, and in a four match Test Series the West Indies won 3-1. They won the second test at Lords, this being the first test the West Indies had won in England. Sonny Ramadhin took 11 wickets in that match and Alf Valentine 7. The calypso's started.

The opening match at Worcester was unfortunately rain affected.

By close of play on day two the West Indies had reached and declared on 249 for 4. F M M Worrell had scored 85, E D Weekes 54, and C L Walcott was 46 not out.

CHAPTER FIVE: THE 1940'S AND 1950'S

Only 58 overs were possible on day three with Worcestershire reaching 134 for 4.

Following the theme of this book, J D C Goddard, F M M Worrell, E D Weekes, C L Walcott, S Ramadhin, along with K B Trestrail, P E W Jones, H H H Johnson, and A F Rae all made their debuts in first class cricket in England.

South Africa opened their 1951 campaign at Worcester on 2, 3 and 4 May.

Worcestershire led by Bob Wyatt won the toss and batted, finally reaching 192 after a weather affected first day. R E Bird scoring 70 not out.

The South Africans replied with 157, Perks taking 4 for 36, Chesterton 3 for 38, and R O Jenkins 3 for 47. Along with Dick Howorth, Worcestershire had a good bowling line up in 1951. George Chesterton was of course a future President of the club and played for the County from 1950 to 1957, taking 263 wickets in his first-class career.

Worcestershire in their second innings had reached 50 for 6 at the close of play on day two, and no play was possible on the final day.

J E Cheetham, D J Mcglew, and W R Endean all made their South African debuts in England in this match.

1952 produced a similar outcome in early May with the visiting Indian tourists.

Only 50 overs of cricket was played on day one, with Worcestershire scoring 101 for 6.

It is interesting to note that Norman Whiting (another future President of the club), and Jack Flavell played in that match.

1952 saw the passing of King George V1, and the accession to the Crown of his eldest daughter Elizabeth. Also, on 7 March, the birth of I V A Richards in Antigua.

1953 Coronation year, as previously mentioned brought an Australian Tour under the Captaincy of A L Hassett, with A R Morris as his Vice Captain. The tour is well documented in Peter West's The fight for the Ashes 1953.

So, the Australians arrived in Worcester and the match was played on 29, 30 April and May 1.

Worcestershire captained by Ronald Bird won the toss and decided to bat.

At the close of play on day one, Worcestershire had reached 243 for 6, Don Kenyon having reached his century, and on day two Worcestershire finally declared on 333 for 7 wickets.

Lindwall had taken 1 wicket, that of Peter Richardson for 0, and Richie Benaud 2 wickets.

J C Hill took 3 wickets, he and Benaud were both debutant spin bowlers, Hill a right arm top spinner, whilst as the world of cricket was to find out Richie Benaud was a fine leg break and googly bowler.

At close of play on day two the tourists had reached 119 for 3, and then enjoyed the final day reaching 542 for 7, to end the match as a draw.

Keith Miller had hit a majestic 220 not out, and G B Hole 112. R G Archer batting at number 8 also scored 108. His first century in first class cricket.

The only consolation for the home team was that J C Whitehead took 5 for 89 on his debut for Worcestershire in first class cricket.

CHAPTER FIVE: THE 1940'S AND 1950'S

Australians G B Hole, C C Mcdonald, R Benaud, G R A Langley , J C Hill , J H Decourcy and R G archer all played their first, first class match in England in this match.

Following the match Don Kenyon was selected to play for England in the first test at Trent Bridge, Nottingham. Opening the batting with Len Hutton, the England captain, Kenyon scored 8, and 16. He retained his place for the second test at Lords, but sadly only scored 3 and 2.

In all he played eight tests for England, but did not enjoy a successful test career, though in first class Cricket we at Worcester know of his phenomenal batting record of 37,002 runs, 74 centuries and 180 half centuries. His captaincy to take us to our first championship in 1964 showed his true character and passion for Worcestershire.

For all English Cricket enthusiasts, the first four tests ended as draws, but England won at the Oval to regain the Ashes for the first time since the bodyline series of 1932/1933.

1954 was again a special season, with the arrival of the first touring party from Pakistan.

The crowd at Worcester, including me, were to witness the first innings of Hanif Mohammed, soon to become the first star of Pakistan Cricket. Known as the Little Master he was to record a 970-minute innings in a test match at Bridgetown Barbados, scoring 337 against the West Indies. A year later he scored the then highest score in first class cricket, playing for Karachi against Bahawalpur, 499 before being run out!

It would be easy to suggest that the whole team played their debut first class match for Pakistan in this country but Maqsood Ahmed was actually the first Pakistan cricketer to play in this country in 1952 playing for the Commonwealth

XI, and A H Kardar, known as the father of Pakistan Cricket actually played for India on their 1946 tour, although he did not play at New Road in that year.

Pakistan won the toss and chose to bat. Although Hanif Mohammed opening only scored 29, the Pakistan team amassed 428, during day two, with Alimuddin and Magsood Ahmed both scoring centuries. The wicket takers for Worcestershire were Perks 3, Flavell 2 and C W Grove 5. C W Grove was a medium fast right arm bowler who was making his debut for Worcestershire having joined the county from Warwickshire.

By the close of play on day two, the home side had been dismissed for 218 in their first innings, with Peter Richardson top scoring with 81. In the second innings Worcestershire were 12 for 0 at stumps.

Worcestershire made a good start with Kenyon 66, Richardson 44 and G Dews 70, before being bowled out for 244.

Fazal Mahmood the Pakistan opening bowler taking 7 for 48 after his first innings haul of 4 for 54.

The visitors had little trouble in scoring the necessary runs to win by 8 wickets.

The Pakistan team played four test matches, and having lost one and drawn two they won the final test at the Oval, where Fazal Mahmood took 12 wickets in the match.

New Road played host to the South Africans on 7, 9 and 10 May 1955.

Worcestershire scored 260 in their first innings, the South Africans replying with 209.

Worcester's second innings totalled 209, leaving the south Africans to score 261 for victory.

CHAPTER FIVE: THE 1940'S AND 1950'S

Excellent bowling by Martin Horton with figures of 9 for 56 reduced the visitors to 143 all out on a very cold day!! It should be noted that H J Tayfield, the South African spin bowler, took 10 wickets in the match as well.

Martin Horton had a long and successful career for Worcestershire, in total playing 410 first class matches, scoring 19,949 runs including 23 centuries and 112 half centuries. He then took 825 first class wickets at 26.94 runs per wicket.

He was briefly recognised by England and played two test matches against India in 1959, scoring 58 in his first innings for England.

T L Goddard, P S Heini, and A R A Murray made their debuts for South Africa in England. The five match test series was much closer with England winning the first two, south Africa the third and fourth and England finally securing the series winning the fifth test.

1956 saw the next Australian touring party under Ian Johnson. They played at New Road on the 2, 3 and 4 May.

As mentioned previously Keith Miller did not play in that match. I had worked out that in his two previous innings he had amassed 270 runs without being out. Had he been out he would have had a higher batting average than Don Bradman even with Bradman's three double centuries and one single century.

Worcestershire won the toss and decided to bat. They were bowled out in 52.1 overs for 90.

Ray Lindwall taking 3 wickets and Richie Benaud 2.

Australia replied with a large 438, and although Flavell and Chesterton took 4 wickets a piece, C C Mcdonald 86, K D Mackay 56 L V Maddocks 56 took Australia forward leaving R Benaud to score 160.

Unfortunately for the Worcester crowd Neil Harvey one of Australia's most talented left handers only scored 2, having toured in both 1948 and 1953. They would see him though in 1961.

The home side's second innings totalled 231 for 9, thus avoiding the innings defeat and the match ended as drawn. Peter Richardson who was captain of the county at that time scored 130 not out which innings led him to a successful Test series, where England retained the Ashes 2 -1.

In his test career of 34 tests, he scored 2,961 at an average of 37.47, with five centuries.

His first-class career for Worcestershire and later Kent totalled 26,055 runs with 44 centuries.

This match recorded the debut for Worcestershire of Roy Booth, and for the Australians, L V Maddocks, W P A Crawford, K D Mackay, and J W Burke.

In the Australian team that match apart from the captain Ian Johnson, there were four other future captains of Australia. Ray Lindwall, Richie Benaud, Neil Harvey and Ian Craig.

Roy Booth had joined Worcestershire from Yorkshire where he had played for his county of birth from 1951 -1955.

In a career spanning 1951-1970 Roy scored 10,134 runs, with two centuries, 24 half centuries, 948 catches and 178 stumpings.

The Ashes were retained by England in 1956, this being the year that Jim Laker took 19 wickets at Old Trafford, and England winning the series 2-1

1957. The West Indies toured England with an exciting line up of new talent and experience. Worcestershire entertained them on 1 and 2 May.

CHAPTER FIVE: THE 1940'S AND 1950'S

Whilst the visiting team contained the experience of C L Walcott, F M M Worrell and A L Valentine, and the debutants G S Sobers, O G "Collie" Smith, D T Dewdney, A G Ganteaume and D S Atkinson, the Worcestershire crowd were not to see the future stars Roy Gilchrist, Wes Hall, and Rohan Kanhai.

As Cricket knows, Collie Smith unfortunately died in 1959, having played 26 tests for the West Indies scoring 1,331 runs including four centuries and 6 half centuries and taking 48 test wickets.

The West Indies under J D C Goddard won the toss and decided to bat, scoring 290 for 9, on day one and declaring overnight. Collie Smith having top scored with 68 and R Berry taking 6 for 105 for the home side.

Worcestershire in reply could only muster 80 in 32.1 overs, Don Kenyon top scoring with 26. Atkinson taking 5 for 25 and Valentine 3 for 11.

Asked to follow on they scored 133 all out, thus being beaten by an innings and 77 runs in two days.

The Test Series was won by England 3-0 with two tests drawn.

1958 the tourists this year were New Zealand. Playing at New Road on 30 April, 1 and 2 May 1958.

The home side won the toss and batted, scoring 345 for 7 declared. A fine century by Peter Richardson 104 was the backbone of the innings. By close of play on day one the visitors were 19 for 2, but a century by B Sutcliffe 139 helped the New Zealand team get to 283. L Coldwell taking 3 for 55.

Worcestershire scored 202 for 4 declared in their second innings, Don Kenyon ending with 102 not out, and Martin Horton 57.

Worcestershire were close to victory at the end of day three with New Zealand 202 for 8 wickets. R Jenkins had taken 4 for 59 and Martin Horton 3 for 50.

7 of the New Zealand team made their first-class debut in England in this match.

On the 29 and 30 April, and the 1 May 1959 Worcestershire entertained the Indian Touring Party.

India under the captaincy of D K Gaekwad had won the toss and chosen to bat.

Their first innings totalled 219, C G Borde scoring 90. D B Pearson taking 4 for 40.

Worcestershire in reply scored 305, with R G Broadbent scoring 102 not out and G Dews 122.

S P Gupte had taken 6 wickets for 92, and R B Desai 4 for 88.

India in their second innings were 157 for 3 at the close. P R Umrigar scoring 87.

An interesting match with C G Borde and R B Desai, amongst six Indian debutants, and D B Pearson being no balled five times for throwing by J S Buller, the umpire.

CHAPTER SIX: 1960 - 1970

The 1960's opened with an opening tourists match against the South Africans, now captained by D J McGlew.

Played on 4, 5 and 6 May 1960, South Africa won the toss and batted, scoring 365 for 6 by the close of play on day one. R A Mclean scored 207 by far the top scorer, though Jack Flavell reducing the South Africans to 28 for 3, had given early hope for the home side. Flavell's figures ended at 3 for 78.

Worcestershire replied with 235, on day two, D W Richardson scoring 72, and J E Pothecary taking 4 for 55, and H J Tayfield 3 for 59.

Day three saw the South Africans declare at 144 for 1 with D J McGlew and T L Goddard both scoring 63, McGlew being not out.

Setting the home side 275 to win Worcestershire could only reach 141 all out. A H McKinnon taking 7 for 42.

England won that Test Series 3 -0 with two drawn.

1961 Worcestershire were visited on 29 April, 1 and 2 May by Richie Benaud's Australians.

A low scoring match but one of huge importance to Worcestershire being the first-class debut of Tom Graveney for the county. So much can be written and has been about one of Worcestershire's most stylish batsmen who joined the county from our neighbours Gloucestershire.

In a career spanning 1948 until 1970, Tom played 79 Tests for England, scoring 4,882 runs with 11 centuries, and 20 half centuries. In his first-class career he scored 47,793 runs at an average of 44.91 per innings, with 122 centuries and 233 half centuries.

Awarded the OBE in 1968 for his services to Cricket, he was President of the MCC in 2004/2005 and of course President of Worcestershire 1994 to 1998.

Worcestershire won the toss and decided to field. The Australians were bowled out for 177, with Martin Horton taking 5 for 46 and Norman Gifford 3 for 42.

The home side replied with 155, Tom Graveney scoring 36 on his debut and Ron Headley 41.

The Australians in their second innings were all out for 141. This time Len Coldwell taking 5 for 45.

Neil Harvey top scoring with 37. In a rain affected match Worcestershire were 56 for 4 at the close. The match being drawn.

An interesting touring party with R B Simpson, A T W Grout, R A Gaunt, N C L O'Neill, F M Misson and B C Booth making their debuts on English soil for their country.

It is noted that the touring party also included W M Lawry, P J P Burge and G D McKenzie.

The Australian team won the Test Series 2-1 to retain the Ashes.

1962 saw the second visit of a team from Pakistan. A drawn match over three days saw Worcestershire winning the toss and batting on day one, scoring 175. Norman Gifford batting at 9, top scored with 41.

By close of play on day one, Pakistan were 97 for 6 and were quickly dismissed for 113.

Mushtaq Mohammad scoring 55 and Flavell and Coldwell taking four wickets a piece.

Worcestershire were dismissed for 245 at the close of play on day two, with Graveney not out on 117.

By the end of the match on day three Pakistan were 291 for 9 wickets, 17 runs short of victory, or for the home side one wicket short of victory.

Among five debutants for Pakistan were Mushtaq Mohammad, who was 86 not out at the close of play, and Intikhab Alam.

England won the five match test series 4-0 in that year.

1963 was quite a year off the pitch, The Beatles arrived, with their first number one record "From Me To You", but more especially they played at the Riverside Dancing Club at Tenbury Wells at the Bridge Inn on 15th April, and then twice at the Gaumont Cinema in Worcester on 28th May and 4th September. To strengthen the Rocking City image, the Rolling Stones also played twice at the Gaumont, on October 9th and December 5th.

1963 saw the West Indies touring side open their first-class tour at Worcester, on the 1, 2 and 3 of May. Unfortunately, very affected by the weather there was no play on day one.

The home side had won the toss and decided to bat. The West Indies bowling attack being W W Hall and CC Griffith, then backed up by G S Sobers and A L Valentine.

Dismissed for 119, with Ron Headley scoring 75 in that total, and Griffith taking 4 for 28, and Valentine 3 for 57, the West Indies responded with 120 for two declared.

C C Hunte 48 not out and B F Butcher 57 not out.

Worcester replied with 162 for 4 declared, and the visitors were 57 for 3 at the close.

C C Griffith made his English first class debut along with E D A S McMorris, B F Butcher, S M Nurse, and D W Allan.

A well-documented Test Series with ever increasing vocal support for the visitors ended with the tourists winning the series 3-1, with C C Griffith being the leading wicket taker with 32 wickets, L Gibbs 26, and G S Sobers 20. W W Hall also took 16.

The leading run scorers in the series were R Kanhai 497 and C C Hunte 471.

This was a very talented touring side under F M M Worrell, with depth in fast and skilful bowling and explosive batting.

Garfield St Aubrun Sobers, a left hand batsman and bowler, became the Wisden Cricketer of the year in 1964 following the 1963 tour. A test career of 93 Tests, 160 innings 8,032 runs at an average of 57.78 with 26 centuries, but also 235 wickets at an average of 34.03.

He was knighted by Queen Elizabeth II, in 1975 for his services to Cricket. His former Captain, Frank Worrell had been similarly knighted in 1964.

1964 was again an Ashes year with the Australians opening first class match at Worcester on 29, 30 April, and 1 May. More importantly for Worcestershire was that it was to be the year we first won the County Championship.

The Australians now captained by Bob Simpson chose to bat and were dismissed on day one for 251. A fine bowling display by Len Coldwell ended with 7 wickets for 53 runs.

A special match as this was the Worcestershire first class debut for Basil D'Oliveira, and also his initial first-class match in England.

He was to represent England in 44 test matches, and in 70 innings he would score 2,484 runs, including 5 centuries, the highest being 158, and he would take 47 test wickets.

CHAPTER SIX: 1960-1970

In his first-class career he would score 19,490 runs with 45 centuries and 551 wickets.

Len Coldwell played 7 tests for England, taking 22 wickets, and in a first-class career he ended with 1,076 wickets. His great opening partner Jack Flavell played 4 tests for England taking 7 wickets but in his first-class career he took 1,529 wickets.

Worcestershire replied with 228, Graveney scoring 56, and D'Oliveira in his first innings 17.

G D McKenzie had taken 5 for 47.

The visitors in their second innings added 196 before declaring, W M Lawry scoring 79, thus leaving Worcestershire 220 to win. In the overs available, the home side secured a draw at 157 for 3 wickets. M J Horton scoring 60.

Worcestershire won their second consecutive Championship title, in 1965 but on the 5, 6, and 7 May they entertained the visiting team from New Zealand.

The visitors batted first and were dismissed for 260. R C Motz batting at 9, scored 95, and gave some respectability to the tourists first innings.

Jack Flavell had excellent bowling figures of 8 wickets for 74 runs.

Worcestershire replied with 255, again Tom Graveney top scoring with 84, and Ron Headley scoring 67.

This had left little time to create a winning position, the New Zealanders scoring 160 for 5 declared, with Flavell taking two more wickets to secure 10 wickets in the match.

The home side ended on 56 for 1 after 18 overs.

Nine of the New Zealand team made their debuts in England in this match.

1966 was of course the World Cup Football year. You all know the result on the 30 July 1966, but on 23 May 1966 Graeme Hick was born in what is now Harare, Zimbabwe.

Worcestershire were again visited by the West Indies team on the 4, 5 and 6 May.

Unfortunately, the weather was atrocious and all that was achieved was the home team making 206 for 7 wickets, with J A Ormrod scoring 72.

The 1967 visitors were India, with a very new look team.

Nine of the team making their debut to England first class cricket. Among these were F M Engineer, D N Sardesia, B S Chandrasekhar, S Venkataraghavan, A L Wadekar and B S Bedi.

The match again was seriously affected by the weather, Worcestershire scoring 335 for 6 on day one, with Basil D'Oliveira scoring 174 not out, and Ron Headley 60. B S Bedi had taken 3 wickets for 68.

There was virtually no play on day two and three with only 44 overs being possible, in which the Indians had scored 106 for 8 wickets. Len Coldwell had taken four wickets for 39 runs.

Pakistan visited New Road in August 1967, a drawn match with Saeed Ahmed scoring 147 in the Pakistan first innings, and in the Worcestershire first innings Tom Graveney was dismissed for 99, and Basil D'Oliveira 96.

In the Pakistan second innings Hanif Mohammad scored 118

The weather was even worse in 1968 for the visiting Australians, the match being abandoned without a ball being bowled.

This tour captained by Bill Lawry, brought Ian Chappell, Ian Redpath, and Doug Walters to the UK. The Test series ended 1-1 and so the Australians retained the Ashes.

CHAPTER SIX: 1960-1970

The story was nearly as bad in 1969 when the West Indians visited Worcester on 3, 4, and 5 May.

The home side now captained by Tom Graveney won the toss and batted, scoring 235 runs for 9 wickets by the close of play on day one. Basil D'Oliveira top scored with 72, and Doug Slade, 57 not out. G C Shillingford making his debut on English soil returned bowling figures of 6 for 63, and his strike bowling partner was Worcester's favourite Vanburn Holder who had joined the county in 1968.

In his career Vanburn played 44 Tests for the West Indies, taking 109 wickets, and in his first-class career 950 wickets.

No play was possible on day two, so Worcestershire declared, the West Indians declared at 87 for 6, on day three, and Worcestershire were 24 for 0 as the match petered out for an inevitable draw.

In 1969 England played a three match Test series with the West Indies, England winning 2 with 1 drawn.

1969 was also the year of the Moon Landing. Apollo 11 with a crew of Neil Armstrong and Buzz Aldrin who made the successful descent and landing, with Michael Collins as the lone Command Module Pilot .

1970 was the controversial year, after the South African Government concerns at the possible selection of Basil D'Oliveira in the MCC Touring party for the 1968/1969 winter tour and the cancellation of that tour because the selectors had added Basil D'Oliveira to the touring party in place of the injured Tom Cartwright. The South African tour of England was cancelled.

An unofficial series took place against a Rest of the World squad.

Accepted as first class matches but not Test Matches it did allow the english cricket loving public to see some of the South African well-known players, in Graeme Pollock, Peter Pollock, Eddie Barlow, Mike Procter, and Barry Richards.

The Rest of the World team, captained by Garfield Sobers, also boasted Farokh Engineer, Lance Gibbs, Rohan Kanhai and Clive Lloyd.

The series had some wonderful centuries, and of course Basil D'Oliveira did represent England.

CHAPTER SEVEN: 1971 - 1979

1971 saw the return of Pakistan to New Road, on 1, 4 May.

Worcestershire captained by Norman Gifford won the toss and chose to bat.

A huge contribution by Glenn Turner of 179 helped the home side finally declare on 305 for 5 and allowing Pakistan to bat in the evening of the first day falter to 35 for 2 at the close. The visitors were finally all out on day 2 for 241, with Zaheer Abbas scoring 110. By the close Worcestershire had taken control of the match ending on 163 for 0.

Worcestershire declared on 251 for 2, with Ron Headley being not out 146, but the visitors batted well throughout their second innings closing on 256 for 6 to draw the match.

Zaheer Abbas, Azmat Rana, and Asif Masood made their first-class debuts in England in this match.

Norman Gifford, a left-hand batsman and slow left arm orthodox bowler captained Worcestershire from 1971-1980, having played for the county from 1960-1982. He then played for Warwickshire from 1983-1988. He played in 15 tests between 1964-1973 taking 33 wickets, and in his first-class career he played 710 matches scored 7,048 runs and took 2,068 wickets. He was awarded the MBE for services to cricket in 1978.

Worcestershire won the John Player Sunday League in 1971.

A strong Australian team under Ian Chappell defeated Worcestershire in two days after no play on day one, on their visit in 1972. There was no play on 29 April, and only 59 overs on day two.

Worcestershire had elected to bat but declared at 98 for 2.

The Australians in their first innings reached 68 for 2 by the close of play and declared overnight.

Worcestershire were dismissed for 99 in 55 overs, with R A L Massie taking 6 for 31, and the visitors scored the necessary 133 for four wickets in 33 overs.

Australian debutants were K R Stackpole, R W Marsh, D J Colley and R A L Massie.

Unfortunately, Dennis Lillee did not make his debut in England at New Road.

The test series was drawn 2-2 and England retained the Ashes.

Worcestershire welcomed New Zealand on 28, 29 and 30 April in 1973.

New Zealand, under B E Congdon, chose to bat and scored 369 for 3 declared. Glenn Turner now opening for New Zealand scored 143, and B E Congdon 93.

The home team replied with 230 all out. R O Collinge taking 6 for 52, and at the close of play on day two the visitors were 26 for 0. Unfortunately no play was possible on day three.

For Worcestershire John Inchmore made his first-class debut.

1974 saw the touring Indian party play their first match at Worcester on 27, 28 and 29 April. Norman Gifford won the toss and decided to bat.

Scoring 258 all out, Basil D'Oliveira scored 108, and Madan Lal took 7 wickets for 95.

India replied with 175 for 9 declared, John Inchmore's bowling attracting much attention with figures of 17.5 overs 7 maidens 4 wickets for 30 runs.

CHAPTER SEVEN: 1971-1979

Worcestershire scored 137 for 4 declared in their second innings, and the Indian tourists were 203 for 6 at the close. S M Gavaskar scoring 88.

Another great year for Worcestershire as we won our third County Championship.

Pakistan were to visit Worcester later in the year but no play was possible on 4, 5 and 6 September.

In 1976 the West Indies played at New Road, but this was on August 18, 19 and 20.

This was one of the most powerful West Indian teams, they won the test series 3-0, and a one-day series by the same margin.

A fast-bowling line up of Andy Roberts, Michael Holding, Wayne Daniel, Bernard Julien, and Vanburn Holder, and batting containing Gordon Greenidge, Roy Fredericks, Alvin Kallicharan, Collis King and Clive Lloyd together with I V A Richards had ruled the season.

Against Worcester, even with Glenn Turner who captained the home side for the match, winning the toss and batting, and scoring 358 for 8 declared on day one, with Phil Neale scoring 143, and Basil D'Oliveira 60, supported by Dipak Patel with 51, the West Indies replied with 408 all out. D'Oliveira taking 4 for 71. And Collis King scoring 109, the West Indian captain Clive Lloyd scoring 73 and Viv Richards 57.

Worcestershire had a torrid second innings being bowled out for 86, Roy Fredericks being the pick of the bowlers with 3 for 10 off 5.5 overs.

The West Indies scored the necessary 38 for 2 to secure victory.

1977 saw Australia visit Worcester but again not as the tour opener. The three-day match on the 28, 29 and 30 May, saw the Australians under Greg Chappell win the toss and decide to bat. At close of play on day one, Australia were 358 all out. Greg Chappell scoring 100 before retiring hurt.

Worcestershire captained by Norman Gifford replied with 243, despite an opening partnership of 114 by Glenn Turner scoring 69 and Alan Ormrod, 73.

The Australians in their second innings declared at 210 for 7, with Norman Gifford taking 4 for 65, and Worcestershire finished the drawn match with 169 for 4. Alan Ormrod scoring his second fifty of the match with 57, a special match for him as he passed 15,000 runs during his first innings and Norman Gifford also took his 1,400th wicket in the second innings.

Bad weather completely ruined the visit of Pakistan in 1978. Only 14 overs of cricket were possible with the visitors scoring 31 for 0.

Worcestershire also played New Zealand on the 19, 20 and 21 August 1978.

A match won by New Zealand by 7 wickets. Worcestershire batting first scoring 193, the visitors replying with 319, J G Wright scoring 65 and G N Edwards 57. Norman Gifford taking 6 wickets for 68.

Our second innings totalled 252, but this allowed the visitors to score 127 for 3 and secure victory. Interestingly in the second innings, all three New Zealand wickets were run outs. R J Hadlee played in this match taking one wicket in each innings.

1979 was again the Prudential World cup year which disrupted the traditional summer timetable, but Worcestershire were visited for the first time for a first-class match by Sri Lanka, on 11, 12 and 13 July.

CHAPTER SEVEN: 1971-1979

The home side captained by E J O Hemsley batted and scored 317 for 6 wickets declared, Basil D'Oliveira scoring 112, and David Humphries, the wicket keeper, 68.

The Sri Lankans scored 264 in reply, with Vanburn Holder now back with Worcestershire taking 3 for 67.

Worcestershire's second innings of 226 for 5 declared contained a fine century of 118 not out by Dipak Patel.

The visitors closed the match on 166 for 1.

It is noted that Tim Curtis and Martin Weston both had their first-class debuts for Worcester in this match.

Tim Curtis played 339 first class matches in his career, including 5 test matches for England. He scored 20,832 first class runs at an average of 40.68, including 43 centuries and 103 half centuries and captained the County from 1992 to 1995.

CHAPTER EIGHT: 1980 - 1999

31st May 1989, Graeme Hick's 100th Hundred, with Vikram Solanki.

The Archbishop of Canterbury

Special Guests. Courtesy of Tim Jones. In the annals of Worcestershire Cricket there is a photograph of Sir Edward Elgar watching cricket at new road. I think the special guests above in this photograph shared the joy of composing and performing music and listening to the cathedral bells at Worcester.

CHAPTER EIGHT: 1980-1999

With Cricket itineraries constantly changing and tours shortening with the demand for touring sides to play both Test Cricket and one day internationals, the traditional curtain raiser at Worcester was becoming less and less, but this book will continue to look at the Tourist first class matches played at New Road, so that the reader can identify the International players who have added so much to our enjoyment of the game in more recent years. Luckily in the 1980's the practice continued and so in 1980 the touring West Indies visited Worcester on 10, 11 and 12 May.

Worcestershire captained by Norman Gifford chose to bat and scored 252 in 82.1 overs. Younis Ahmed top scoring with 43. Messrs Croft, Marshall and Garner took 6 wickets between them, and D R Parry 4 for 55. In the time available on the first evening, the home side with our own West Indian attack initially reduced the visitors to 7 for 3. With Hartley Alleyne, our overseas player from Barbados, and Vanburn Holder also originally from Barbados, it must have been exciting first overs. Gordon Greenidge bowled Alleyne 1, Desmond Haynes lbw b Alleyne 0, and Viv Richards bowled Holder 5.

The Visitors recovered on day 2 to 266 all out, with Kallicharran scoring 89 and Marshall 52. Alleyne had finished with bowling figures of 4 for 83, and Holder 3 for 67.

Worcestershire in their second innings buckled to an onslaught from Malcolm Marshall being 144 all out. Marshall taking 7 for 56. The West Indies scored 134 for 3 to win the match, and whilst Greenidge scored 60 and Haynes 41, Dipak Patel has caught and bowled Viv Richards for 0 before the winning runs were scored.

The match recorded the debut of D L Haynes, S F A F Bacchus and D R Parry to first class cricket in England.

Worcestershire were visited by Sri Lanka for a first-class match on 1, 2 and 3 July 1981.

Sri Lanka later that year were awarded Test Match status and played their first Test Match against England in February 1982 at Colombo.

Worcestershire scored 301 all out and the Sri Lankans' replied with 350.

The home side's second innings totalled 225 for 6 at close of play. Mark Scott had scored 73 and Dipak Patel 72.

Later that month New Road was visited by Australia.

Captained by Kim Hughes, Australia put the home side into bat and bowled us out for 189. R M Hogg doing the early damage with 3 for 42.

The visitors replied with 293 and Worcestershire saw for the first time the batting of Allan Border, with 115. Jim Cumbes had taken 4 for 62.

Worcestershire in their second innings witnessed a fine innings of 145 not out by our skipper Phil Neale, finally declaring on 344 for 8 wickets.

The Australians however scored the necessary 241 for 3 wickets in 33.4 overs. G M Wood scoring 59 and A R Border 70 not out, with D M Wellham 54 not out.

England retained the Ashes that year winning 3 tests to 1, with one drawn.

In 1982 Worcestershire entertained both Pakistan and Zimbabwe in first class matches. The Zimbabweans visited New Road on 2, 3 and 4 June, the very first, first class match played by Zimbabwe in England but time was lost to bad

CHAPTER EIGHT: 1980-1999

weather with the home side reaching 117 for 3 at the close of day one and declaring at 222 for 9 wickets on day two. Martin Weston opening had scored 63 and Younis Ahmed 63.

A J Traicos had taken 5 for 57.

Zimbabwe replied with 156 for 3 wickets at the close of play on day two, A J Pycroft 62 not out and D A G Fletcher 56 not out. Worcestershire in their second innings scored 181 for 7 before declaring, Younis Ahmed scoring 75 not out, and P W E Rawson taking 5 for 42.

Zimbabwe were 52 for2 at the close.

On the 10, 11, and 12 July the County played Pakistan, captained by Imran Khan, who had played for Worcestershire 1971-1976.

Worcestershire having scored 188 all out with Phil Neale, the captain scoring 68, and D J Humphries 46, met with the Tourists posting 467 for 4 declared.

Mohsin Khan retiring hurt on 165, Zaheer Abbas scoring 147, and Mudassar Nazar 75.

The opening partnership had achieved 164.

Worcester replied with 186, Iqbal Qasim taking 5 for 52, and Abdul Qadir 4 for 75.

Only Martin Weston with 93, and Phil Neale with 59 making any contribution to save the match.

Imran Khan played 88 Test Matches between 1971 and 1991/92, scoring 6 centuries and taking 362 wickets.

As a footnote Glenn Turner had left Worcestershire at the end of the 1982 season.

His playing career spanned 1964 to 1983 during which he scored 2,991 runs in 41 test matches for New Zealand, including 7 centuries. The highest score being 259.

His first-class career amassed 34,346 runs at an average of 49.7. This included 103 centuries and 148 half centuries. A further 10,784 runs in List A which included 14 more centuries.

In 1983 Worcestershire entertained New Zealand on 20, 21 and 22 July and in an entertaining match New Zealand batting first scored 246 all out. M D Crowe made 65 and R G Hadlee 68. John Inchmore took 5 wickets for 82.

The home side responded with 200 all out. Basil D'Oliveira scoring 77 and M S A McEvoy 54.

New Zealand declared their second innings at 210 for 6, and then bowled Worcestershire out comfortably in 35.3 overs. R J Hadlee taking 4 for 42.

Whilst New Road welcomed the visiting West Indies team, captained by Viv Richards, I am taking this opportunity to say 1984 was a very special season for Worcestershire which would bolster the club into the 21st Century. Worcestershire welcomed a young Zimbabwean cricketer on a scholarship from the Zimbabwean Cricket Union.

Graeme Hick had already played first class cricket in Zimbabwe and was considered more a bowler than a batsman. At the age of 16, he had already dismissed Dean Jones in a Zimbabwe Colts match against Young Australia and played against David Boon and in his initial first-class match for Zimbabwe in October 1983 at the Harare Sports Club also playing against a young West Indies team featuring Courtney Walsh. They were to meet many times again!!

Graeme in that match scored 28 not out.

In 1984, playing for Kidderminster in the Birmingham league, he scored 1,234 runs and played his first match for Worcestershire at the Oval on 8 September 1984.

CHAPTER EIGHT: 1980-1999

He did not bat in the first innings but top scored in the second innings with 82 not out.

Graeme will repeatedly come up in this book from now on, but I will summarise his contribution to Worcestershire and England Cricket now.

65 Test Matches, 114 Innings, 3,383 runs at an average of 31.32, 6 hundreds and 18 fifties, 23 wickets and 90 catches

His ODI career 120 matches, 118 innings, 3,846 runs average 37.33, 5 hundreds and 27 fifties 64 catches, and 30 wickets.

His first-class career 871 innings, 41,112 runs at an average 52.23 with a highest score of 405 not out, 136 centuries and 158 fifties. 709 catches, 232 wickets.

List A cricket 630 innings, 22,059 runs, 40 centuries, 139 fifties, 289 catches and 225 wickets.

And finally, just as T20 was starting to be part of the Cricket Summer 36 innings, 1,201 runs, 2 centuries 10 fifties, 10 catches.

We must not forget 6 May 1988, when he scored his 405 not out at Taunton, 28 May 1988, when he scored his 1,000th run before the end of May, and 31 May 1998 when he scored his 100th Century against Sussex.

But getting back to the visit of the West Indies Tourists in 1984.

Following on from the reference to Courtney Walsh playing for the Young West Indies in Zimbabwe in 1983, Courtney Walsh made his debut for the West Indies in England at Worcester in this match.

A wonderful right arm fast bowler he was to play in 132 test matches and whilst only scoring 936 runs he would take 519 Test wickets at an average of 24.44, with 22 five wicket hauls and ten wickets in a test match 3 times.

A first-class career of 1,807 wickets and a one-day test career of 227 wickets. A total List A career of 551 wickets.

The West indies captained by Viv Richards won the toss and decided to bat.

By the second day they declared on 412 for 9 wickets. Greenidge had scored 138 and Haynes 89. They had achieved an opening partnership of 206.

Worcestershire in reply had reached 124 for 1, with T S Curtis 82 not out, but the weather ensured little play was possible on day three.

Facing a bowling line up of Walsh, Garner, Holding, Baptiste and Harper must have been a daunting task.

Debuts in England were made by R B Richardson, A L Logie, P J L Dujon and C A Walsh.

In the matches against England, the West Indies beat England 2-1 in a one-day series and in the test series beat England 5-0.

The West Indies were showing their dominance in World Cricket, with exceptional bowling, adding Malcolm Marshall to the above list

The scorecards make exceptional reading with Greenidge scoring two double centuries and other West Indian batsmen scoring individual centuries, Richards, Dujon, Gomes and Haynes. The bowlers took it in turns to destroy the England replies, Garner in the first, Marshall in the second, Holding and Marshall in the third, Garner and Harper in the fourth, Marshall and Holding in the fifth.

Richie Richardson and Courtney Walsh could not get into the Test Team this tour, although Richardson did play in two of the one day internationals.

CHAPTER EIGHT: 1980-1999

Richardson went on to Captain the West Indies, and in his test career played 86 tests, 146 innings scoring 5,949 runs including 16 hundreds and 27 fifties.

In a first-class career he scored 14,618 runs, 37 centuries and 68 half centuries.

The Australians visited Worcester on the 11, 12 and 13 May 1985 but this was not the tour opening fixture.

Again, Phil Neale captaining Worcestershire and batting first scored 108 in a first innings total of 303 for 6 declared.

The Australians captained by Allan Border replied with 364 for 5 declared, Border himself scoring 135, and David Boon 73 not out. John Inchmore had taken 3 for 38.

Worcestershire were 93 for 4 at the close in a drawn match.

Six test matches were played in 1985, England winning the series 3-1, and retaining the Ashes.

1985 was a special year for me and my connection with the club, as John Inchmore asked me to be his Benefit Treasurer. It was a fun year, and we raised some £46,000 in the Benefit season.

John was a committed and respected team member from 1973-1986, very popular with the members and his teammates, taking 510 first class wickets in his career and scoring 3,137 runs.

That included one century against Essex in 1974 when he had the opportunity starting his innings as the night watchman.

The Indians opened their tour at Worcester in 1986 on the 6, 7 and 8 May.

The Indians under Kapil Dev asked Worcester to bat and at the close of play on day one the home side were 230 for 9 wickets, at which they declared overnight.

Graeme Hick had scored 70. The Indian team replied with 297 all out. M Azharuddin had scored 76 and Kapil Dev 51. Worcester had scored 56 for 0 at the close of day two but no play was possible on the third day.

Six Indian cricketers made their debut for India in this match, including K Srikkanth, M Prabhakar, and M Azharuddin, and of course Kapil Dev had been Worcestershire's overseas player in 1984/85.

In all he played 131 tests, scoring 8 centuries and taking 434 wickets 1978/79-1993/94.

Pakistan visited Worcester in July 1987, won the toss, batted and on day one scored 304 for 1 wicket.

Shoaib Mohammad scored 121 not out and Mansoor Akhtar 169 not out.

There was little play on day two, and by the close of play on the third day Worcester had reached 275 for three.

Damian D'Oliveira top scored with 131 not out and Phil Neale was 69 not out.

Worcestershire won the Refuge Assurance League in 1987.

1988 The West Indians were back at New Road on the 28, 29 and 30 May 1988.

In a rain affected game, Worcestershire had been put into bat by Viv Richards and by close of play on day one the home side were 284 for 1. Gordon Lord being out for 0, bowled Ambrose, Worcestershire had then put on 284 for the second wicket, with Tim Curtis 78 not out and Graeme Hick 172 not out. The significance of this day's cricket was that when Graeme reached 153, he had scored 1,000 first class runs by the end of May. Five days after his 22nd birthday. And against Patterson, Ambrose, Walsh and Bishop.

CHAPTER EIGHT: 1980-1999

This had been achieved by W G Grace in 1895, Tom Hayward of Surrey in 1900, Walter Hammond of Gloucestershire in 1927, and Charlie Hallows of Lancashire in 1928. Donald Bradman achieved it twice in 1930 and 1938, Bill Edrich of Middlesex also achieved it in 1938.

Since the second World War it has only been achieved twice, by Glenn Turner in 1973 and finally Graeme in 1988.

It is interesting to note that Brian Lara came very close achieving it on 2nd June 1994, and also Zaheer Abbas on the 4 June in 1971.

Worcestershire declared on day two at 321 for 3, when Tim Curtis had scored 82 and Graeme Hick 172, as no further play was possible on that day.

On the third day, the West Indies ended on 170 for five after 54 overs. D L Haynes had scored 71 and I V A Richards 50.

Whilst England won the one-day series 3-0 the West Indies won the Test Series 4-0 with one drawn, very much due to the accurate bowling of Marshall and Ambrose.

Worcestershire won both the County Championship and the Refuge Assurance League in 1988.

1989 had an interesting match with the visiting Australians. The season opener for the Australians, saw them under Allan Border win the toss, and decide to bat on 13 May, to be all out in 30.5 overs for 103. Phil Newport taking 6 wickets for 43 runs in 10.5 overs.

The scorecard makes interesting reading.

G R Marsh 21, M A Taylor 6, T M Moody 9, A R Border 8, M R J Veletta 0, S R Waugh 0, I A Healy 25 no, T V Hohns 3, G F Lawson 8, M G Hughes 2, and T M Alderman 6. Extras 15.

Worcestershire however were similarly bowled out on the same day for 146.

Captained by Ian Botham, who scored 39, with Tim Curtis making the only other contribution of 46.

Alderman had taken 4 for 33, and Lawson 3 for 50.

The Australians were already 51 for 4 in their second innings at the close of play but managed to extend their second innings to 205.

Steve Waugh scored 63, and Allan Border 48. Phil Newport taking a further 5 wickets for 84 and Neil Radford 4 for 58.

Setting Worcester 163 to win, the target was reached with seven wickets down on day two. Graeme Hick scoring 43, and I T Botham 42.

The match saw Australian debuts for T M Moody, M A Taylor, T V Hohns, I A Healy, M R J Veletta and G R Marsh.

The six match test series saw the Australians regain the Ashes, the first time since 1982/1983. M A Taylor the leading batsman for Australia with 839 runs in the series, and Alderman the leading bowler with 41 wickets.

During the series, Ian Botham, Tim Curtis, Phil Newport and Graham Dilley were all selected for various Tests.

Phil Newport in his career represented England in 3 tests, taking 10 wickets, and scoring 110 runs. In his career he took 880 first class wickets.

Worcestershire went on to win the County Championship in 1989.

Tom Moody became a great favourite at Worcestershire thereafter, both as an attacking batsman but later as the team coach and Director of Cricket. He captained Worcestershire from 1995-1999.

CHAPTER EIGHT: 1980-1999

Surprisingly he only played in 8 Test matches, and in 14 innings scored 456 runs with two centuries and three 50's. He only took two wickets at Test Level.

His One Day International career was however more successful, as an all-rounder he scored 1,211 runs in 64 innings with 10 half centuries and took 52 wickets.

In his first-class career he scored 64 centuries.

Mark Taylor took over Captaincy of Australia after Allan Border from 1994 to 1999.

In 104 test matches and 186 innings, he scored 7,525 runs averaging 43.49, with his highest test score 334 not out in Pakistan in 1998. Having equalled Donald Bradman's highest score, Taylor declared. He scored 19 test centuries and 40 half centuries.

In One-Day Internationals, he scored a further 3,514 runs in 110 innings, with 1 century and 28 fifties.

In 1990, New Road entertained the New Zealand team on 12, 13 and 14 May for their tour opener.

J G wright captaining the New Zealanders won the toss and asked Worcestershire to bat.

The home side were bowled out in 61 overs for 171, only Damian D'Oliveira and Stuart Lampitt making meaningful contributions of 48 and 40 respectively. Graeme Hick had retired hurt for 2 and took no further part in the game. Richard Hadlee had taken 5 for 27.

By close of play the visitors were in trouble at 113 for 8, but again thanks to Richard Hadlee with 90 they recovered to be all out 201.

Phil Newport had taken 6 for 54 and in Worcestershire's second innings, he excelled again, this time with the bat in scoring 98, with Richard Illingworth scoring 74 and Worcestershire totalling 274.

This was to be Phil's highest first-class score.

New Zealand having been set 245 to win, achieved this for 4 wickets, with a first wicket stand of 163, T J Franklin scoring 50 and J G Wright 99. Richard Illingworth taking 3 for 35.

A H Jones, D K Morrison, J P Millrow, and M W Priest made their debuts for New Zealand in England.

In 1991, the West Indians under Viv Richards opened their tour at New Road, on 15, 16, and 17 May.

The West Indies chose to bat and by day two had reached 409 for 7 before declaring.

Phil Simmons had made 134 and Viv Richards 131.

Worcestershire replied with 288, containing 161 by Ian Botham. Walsh and Patterson taking 3 wickets each. The match ended in a draw with the West Indies 36 for 0.

This was the match that Brian Lara made his first-class debut in England, together with I B A Allen.

Lara, a left-hand batsman from Trinidad, was to represent the West Indies in 130 Tests, scoring 11,912 runs in 230 innings, at an average of 53.17, 34 centuries, 48 half centuries. Highest score 400 not out (scored against England at St Johns, Antigua, in 2004).

His one-day career for the West Indies covered 295 matches, 10,348 runs, 19 centuries and 62 half centuries.

In all first class matches he scored 22,156 runs with 65 centuries averaging 51.88.

One has to remember his highest score of 501 not out, in 1994, for Warwickshire v Durham.

CHAPTER EIGHT: 1980-1999

And in list A, a total of 14,602 runs, with 27 centuries.

Worcestershire in 1991 won both the Benson & Hedges Cup and the Refuge Assurance Trophy.

It was also the long-awaited year that Graeme Hick finally qualified to play for England.

He played in all three one day internationals which England won 3-0 and four of the five tests, the series being drawn 2-2.

I will not add to the many articles on Graeme's Test Career, except to say the standard of World fast bowling at that time, especially the West Indies, Australia and South Africa (once they came back into the Test Arena) was extremely high and hostile.

The Pakistan Tourists visited Worcester on 6, 7 and 8 May for their tour opener, and under the captaincy of Salim Malik, they decided to bat and had a good first day, scoring 374 for 4 declared. Rameez Raja opening the batting scoring 172, with 28 fours before being caught and bowled by Richard Illingworth.

Richard went on to play 9 test matches for England 1991-1995/1996, taking 19 wickets and 30 wickets in 25 one day internationals. In his first-class career he took 831 wickets.

Saleem Malik added 91.

By the close on day one, Worcestershire were 43 for 0, and they declared on day two at 303 for 5. Tim Curtis captaining Worcester had scored 85, with Philip Weston 64 not out and Steve Rhodes 4 not out.

Amazingly Pakistan were bowled out on the final day for 93.

Phil Newport taking 5 for 22.

Worcestershire had 56 overs to score the necessary 166 runs to win the match with again Tim Curtis scoring 45, Grame Hick 33 and Philip Weston 32 not out.

Interesting debutants were Rashid Latif, Inzamam-ul-Haq, Aamer Sohail, and Mushtaq Ahmed.

1993 saw the Australians play at New Road, again the traditional opening first class match.

The visitors captained by Mark Taylor although the Tour Captain was Allan Border, won the toss and batted, but were bowled out before the close of play on day one for 262, even though D C Boon had scored 108 and Steve Waugh 49 not out. Mark Taylor had opened and scored 39. Worcestershire though only replied with 90, and extras were top scorer with 21.

Following on though, Worcestershire scored 458 for 4 declared, a well-documented session of play when Graeme Hick scored 187, with 8 sixes and 24 fours and Shane Warne bowling 23 overs for 1 wicket and 122 runs taken from him. Shane was not going to show Graeme his full repertoire just yet.

Tim Curtis scored 67 and Stuart Lampitt and Steve Rhodes ending on 68 not out.

Worcestershire could not secure victory as the Australians scored 287 for five to win the match. David Boon scoring his second century of the match with 106, and Matthew Hayden 96 led the way to a fine run chase.

Could I believe it when I checked to see that Shane Warne, and Matthew Hayden were first class debutants for Australia in England on our beloved square. Two more great names to add to the list.

Also, first matches for P R Reiffel, B P Julian, and W J Holdsworth.

CHAPTER EIGHT: 1980-1999

The six match Test Series was comprehensively won by Australia 4-1, and the 3 match one day series similarly 3-0.

The Australians thus retained the Ashes.

It is a pleasure to recite the test Career of Shane Warne.

He played in 145 tests scored 3,154 runs in 199 innings, and sadly his highest test score was 99. He scored 12 half centuries. Bowling his leg breaks and googlies accounted for 708 wickets. His best 8 for 71, 5 wickets in an innings 37 times, and 10 wickets in a Test Match 10 times. In his one-day international career for Australia he took a further 291 wickets.

Matthew Hayden played 103 Test matches for Australia and in 184 innings scored 8,625 runs at an average of 50.73. His highest score being 380, and he achieved 30 centuries and 29 half centuries. He was similarly a successful member of the One Day International team with 160 appearances, 154 innings 6131 runs at an average of 44.10 including 10 centuries, the highest being 181 not out, and 36 half centuries.

We now move into 1994. A year when Worcestershire won the NatWest trophy.

But first the New Zealanders opened their first-class tour on 4, 5 and 6 May. Having won the toss, they asked the home side to bat and after 87.5 overs during day two Tim Curtis declared with Worcestershire on 343 for 7. Steve Rhodes had scored 100 not out, Graeme Hick 67 and Gavin Haynes 82.

The visitors replied with 194 for 7 declaring early on day three. K R Rutherford the captain scoring 84. Worcestershire then batted for 21 overs scoring 103 for 6 before declaring with Grame Hick scoring 38. Setting the New Zealanders an unlikely 253 to win the match ended as a draw with the tourists scoring 153 for 4.

The match marked the debuts of five New Zealand Cricketers.

1995 brought the West Indies to Worcester, still as the tour opener, but bad weather wrecked the prospect of a competitive match. Play on the 16 May was limited to West Indians, now captained by Richie Richardson, only being able to score 114 for 2.

They declared after a total of 65.3 overs for 241 for 9 on day three as no play had been possible on day two. Brian Lara had top scored with 78.

P A Thomas had taken 5 for 70.

Worcestershire forfeited their first innings and the visitors their second, but in 26.3 overs that were possible the home side had reached 86 for five.

There were debuts for J R Murray, S Chanderpaul, S C Williams, R Dhanraj, and S L Campbell

Shivnarine Chanderpaul, a left-hand bat played in 164 Tests for the West Indies, and in 280 innings scored 11,867 runs, 30 centuries with a highest score of 203 not out, and 66 half centuries. In one-day internationals he added a further 8,778 runs in 268 matches, a further 11 centuries and 59 half centuries.

I also notice that Jimmy Adams played for the West Indies. He had played his first, first-class match in this Country playing in a first-class festival match in Scarborough for the Presidents XI so his innings may well have been his first playing for the West Indies in this country. His 54 test matches and 90 innings enabled him to score 3,012 runs including six centuries and 14 fifties with a highest score of 208 not out against New Zealand in 1995/1996 at Antigua.

He also took 27 wickets and took over the captaincy of the West Indies from Brain Lara in 2000.

CHAPTER EIGHT: 1980-1999

1996 was a fun year at Worcestershire CCC. Steve Rhodes Benefit Year and Steve had asked me to be the Benefit Treasurer. Some fun events and in total raising £167,025.

Steve played 11 tests for England, scoring 294 runs with a highest score of 65 no.

More importantly he took 46 catches and 3 stumpings.

He also played in 9 one day internationals scoring 107 runs and taking 9 catches and 2 stumpings. In First class cricket 440 matches, 14,839 runs, 12 centuries and 72 fifties. 139 catches and 124 stumpings.

So 1996, after a ten year absence, Worcestershire entertained the Indian Tourists at New Road.

Again, the tour opened on the 8, 9 and 10 May 1996.

This would be the first time a Worcester crowd would see Sachin Tendulkar batting for India, though he had experienced his first-class cricket in 1990 on the shortened tour that year which did not include a match at New Road.

I think it would be remiss not to mention his international career of 200 tests between 1989/1990 and 2013/2014, 329 innings 15,921 runs 51 centuries with a highest score of 248 not out and 68 fifties.

He also took 46 wickets and in his one-day international career a further 18,426 runs in 463 matches with 49 centuries and 96 half centuries. Also 154 wickets with his right arm, off break and leg break bowling, but also as a right arm medium pace bowler.

As to the match at New Road, India won the toss and decided to bat, declaring before the close of play on 349 for 5. V Rathour the opener scoring 165, Tendulkar 52 and Azharuddin 68.

Worcestershire replied with 476 for 6 declared on the morning of the third day.

Graeme Hick had scored 215 in an innings of 233 minutes with 30 fours and 6 sixes. Philip Weston had scored 98 and Steve Rhodes 53. In the remaining 68 overs of day three India had reached 340 for 2. A D Jadeja scoring 105 not out and V Rathour 72.

Five Indians, S C Ganguly, A D Jadeja, B K V Prasad, V Rathour and P L Mhambrey debuted for their country in this match.

Again, I should briefly detail Sourav Ganguly's Test and One Day International Career.

113 Tests, 7,212 runs in 188 innings, 16 centuries, his highest score being 239 and 32 wickets. An ODI Career of 308 matches, 11,221 runs, 22 centuries, 71 fifties and 100 wickets.

Worcestershire also entertained the visiting South Africa A team in August 1996 in a four-day match at New Road.

Briefly the visitors won the toss and batted, and on day one, they were all out for 202 in 49.2 overs. J B Commins the captain scoring 61. The home side in reply scored 77 all out in 20.5 overs. G M Gilder taking 8 wickets for 22 runs.

By close of play on day one, South Africa A were 160 for 6.

They managed to extend their second innings score to 325, with an innings of 105 by M W Pringle. Worcestershire were 96 for 3 at the close of play on day two, and 239 for 6 by close of play on day three, the weather affecting this game on the two days. Finally on the last day the home side were bowled out for 278 and the visitors had won by 172 runs.

In the second innings David Leatherdale had scored 73 and Steve Rhodes 51.

CHAPTER EIGHT: 1980-1999

In the South Africa A side were H H Gibbs, and P R Adams.

In the Worcestershire team was one young cricketer who I had watched at school level. Scott Ellis. The scorecard reads in the South Africa A second innings "H H Gibbs Ct Ralph Bowled Ellis 5." A memorable scalp. Scott Ellis played 12 first class matches taking 20 wickets. 1995-1998.

In 1997 Worcestershire played a fifty over game against Australia, and a first-class match against a touring Pakistan A side. A three-day match in July of 1997 ended in a draw.

Worcestershire were put in to bat and made 265, Graeme Hick 55 and Gavin Haynes 65.

Pakistan A replied with 489 for 9 declared. Saleem Elahi scoring a magnificent 229, and Mohammed Wasim the captain 64. Farhan Adil also added 50.

Worcestershire replied with 338 for 4 by the end of the match. Graeme Hick scoring 144

The visitors in 1998 after many years of absence were South Africa. Led by W J "Hansie" Cronje they were to record a series win in three one day internationals 2-1 but lost the test series 2-1.

At Worcester on the 14, 15 and 16 of May the visitors won the toss and batted and scored 287 for 4 declared on day one, with G F J Liebenburg scoring 98, J H Kallis 75, and D J Cullinan 67 not out.

Worcestershire replied with 228 for six declared. David Leatherdale scoring 69, Steve Rhodes 45 and Graeme Hick 33. Lance Klusener had taken 4 for 66.

The South African second innings totalled 219 for 6 declared with J H Kallis scoring 74, and G Kirsten 51.

Worcestershire in their fourth innings made 189 all out even though Graeme Hick made 58, A Donald taking 6 for 56, led the South Africans to a victory by 89 runs.

Hansie Cronje played 68 test matches for South Africa 1991/1992 - 1999/2000, and Jacques Kallis recorded 45 centuries in his test career.

On that theme, remember on 31st May 1998 Graeme Hick scored his 100th first class century against Sussex on 31 May.

Worcestershire were due to play New Zealand for a four-day 1st Class match on the 9 to 12 June, but the match was cancelled as New Zealand had qualified for the Super Six Stage of the World Cup.

1999 was of course the centenary year of Worcestershire becoming a first-class county and the visiting Australians played a one-day match to commemorate the Centenary.

Prince Philip, the Duke of Edinburgh was the guest of honour at that match.

Worcestershire also played a visiting Sri Lanka A team for a four-day match in August.

Day one was lost because the visitors kit and luggage was lost on the airflight, and the start of day two was delayed because of an Eclipse of the sun!

1999 was also Graeme Hick's benefit year. With a committee chaired by the late Cecil Duckworth CBE, I was asked to be Treasurer, and with Jenny Lazenby as Secretary and Cynthia Crawford MBE on the committee, we with all the other committee members and helpers had a great year of events (some in some strange places), but Graeme and Jackie enjoyed the whole year. Graeme was awarded the MBE in 2009.

CHAPTER NINE: 2000 ONWARDS

So, we move to the 21st Century, to see Cricket evolve to Franchise Cricket and the IPL, The Hundred and the financial direction to the shorter forms of Cricket.

I aimed to keep this book focussed on first class cricket played at New Road, and so India played their last first-class match at Worcester in 2002, the West Indies in 2000, South Africa in 1998, Pakistan via their A team 1997, and New Zealand 2004. Zimbabwe 2003, Australia amazingly 2019, and Sri Lanka A 1999.

In 2000, we were visited by the West Indies and in a first-class match and a West Indian debut in this country for a great West Indian who could fill stadiums, I accept more in one day internationals and that was C H Gayle. It was also the debut match for C D Collymore, M V Nagamootoo, W Phillip, R R Sarwan, and A F C Griffith.

The match details were that West Indies won the toss and batted, but were all out in 62.2 overs for 164 runs. Chris Gayle actually top scoring with 38.

Worcestershire responded with 232, Vikram Solanki hitting 51. The West Indies in their second innings batted through the third day scoring 301 for 9. S Chanderpaul scoring an unbeaten 161.

Christopher Henry Gayle. 103 Test Matches, 182 innings, 7,214 runs, 15 centuries and 37 Fifties. His highest Test Score being 333 against Sri Lanka, at the Galle International Stadium, in November 2010.

He took 73 test wickets.

In his one-day international career for the West indies in 298 matches and 291 innings he scored 10,425 runs, 25 hundreds, 53, fifties and took 167 wickets.

In all List A cricket, he scored 13,193 runs with 29 hundreds and 70 half centuries.

He even hit 2 centuries in International twenty 20 cricket, scoring in total 1,899 runs in 79 appearances. And took 20 wickets.

In all T20 cricket he scored 14,562 runs in 463 matches, including 22 centuries and 88 fifties, with 83 wickets.

Many will remember the 2005 season when he joined Worcestershire as our Overseas player.

He captained the West Indies from 2007 to 2010.

The year 2000 also saw Kidderminster Harriers join the Football League. A Brilliant Achievement.

The Australian tourists continued the tradition of opening their first-class tour in 2001 on the 1, 2 and 3 June.

Under Steve Waugh the Australians chose to bat and scored 351 all out on day one. D R Martyn scored 108 primarily supported by Shane Warne 68.

The home team replied with 163 all out. A Singh making 62.

Glenn McGrath returning to New Road after playing for Worcestershire in 2000, continued his fine bowling on the Worcester square with 3 for 31.

The visitors in their second innings scored 360 for 8 wickets declared, with only Hayden 65 and Ponting 65, exceeding 50.

The home team were bowled out on day three for 188, with David Leatherdale the main scorer with 72.

Again, McGrath had taken 4 for 31.

CHAPTER NINE: 2000 ONWARDS

This was a strong Australian team with both Steve and Mark Waugh in the side alongside M L Hayden, R T Ponting, D R Martyn, A C Gilchrist, S K Warne, D W Fleming, N W Bracken and G D McGrath, but interestingly in 1995 Worcestershire had played a first class fixture against Young Australia, and who was playing in that match. M L Hayden, J L Langer, A C Gilchrist and R T Ponting who posted 103 not out.

Needless to say, The Australians won the test Series 4 -1, with Glenn McGrath the leading wicket taker in the series with 32 wickets, Shane Warne with 31 and Mark Waugh the leading Australian batsman with 430 runs, thus retaining the Ashes which they had held since 1989.

Ricky Ponting scored 13,378 runs in 168 tests, 287 innings, with 41 centuries and 62 half centuries. In one day internationals, a further 13,589 runs in 364 innings with 29 centuries.

India visited New Road for a first class four-day game in 2002.

With no play on the first two days and under S C Ganguly, India won the toss and batted, and the Worcestershire crowd were witness to Sachin Tendulkar scoring 169 (with 30 fours), and R S Dravid 53 not out, in a first innings of 417 for 8 declared.

Worcestershire replied with 200 for six at the close of day four.

Worcestershire entertained Zimbabwe in 2003, a four-day game from the 9 to 12 May.

An interesting match with the home side now captained by Ben Smith choosing to bat and reaching 262 all out. Vikram Solanki scored 74, and Ben Smith 53.

The Zimbabwean visitors replied admirably with 334 all out. S V Carlisle making 157.

Worcestershire were then bowled out for 247, leaving Zimbabwe needing 176 to win.

The visitors were bowled out for 175, making this a memorable tie. Kabir Ali taking 5 for 48.

Andrew Hall, a South African from the Transvaal, making his debut in this country for Worcestershire scored 68 in the Worcester second innings, and S D Peters 63.

Andrew Hall played 21 tests for South Africa, scoring 760 runs, one century of 163 and 3 fifties, and took 45 test wickets.

In 88 appearances for South Africa in one day internationals he took 95 wickets.

R W Price made his debut in England alongside T J Friend, for Zimbabwe.

He subsequently played for Worcestershire 2004-2007 and played in 22 Test Matches for Zimbabwe taking 80 wickets.

2004 New Road welcomed the touring New Zealand team to a four-day match on 7, 8, 9, and 10 May.

Worcestershire scored 270 for 9 declared, Ben Smith the captain scoring 92, and New Zealand replied with 379 for 7 declared. J D P Oram scoring 103 not out and C D McMillan 86.

Worcestershire in their second innings now saw the best of Graeme Hick with 204 not out, with 8 sixes and 27 fours. The home side declared on 318 for 6, and the match ended with the visitors 77 for 1.

In moving quickly to 2005, we should firstly record that Worcester Warriors joined the Premiership in 2004.

There are now three remaining first class matches against touring sides to comment on. All three were against Australia, 2005, 2013, and 2019, and none were tour openers.

CHAPTER NINE: 2000 ONWARDS

2005 saw Worcestershire win the toss and put Australia in to bat in a three day fixture.

The tourists duly scored 406 for 9 declared. Runs for J L Langer 54, M L Hayden 79, J B J Haddin 94 and J N Gillespie 53 not out.

Worcestershire replied with 187 in 44 overs. S C Moore scoring 69, and M S Kaprowicz taking 5 for 67.

The Australians were 161 for 2 at the end of the match. M J Clarke scoring 59 and R T Ponting, the captain, 59 not out.

This was the year that England finally won back the Ashes by winning the series 2-1.

2009 was a four-day game in July, the Australians now captained by Michael Clarke, won the toss, batted and scored 396 for 4 in their first innings. S R C Watson 109, C J L Rogers 75, E J M Cowan 58, M J Clarke 62 and S P D Smith 68 not out, and Phil Hughes 19 not out. How tragic that Phil Hughes would die in 2014, hit by a bouncer in an Australian Shield match in Sydney. Worcestershire enjoyed his cricket for the county in 2012. He played in 26 test matches, scoring 1,535 runs in 49 innings, with 3 centuries and 7 half centuries.

Worcestershire had also welcomed Steve Smith as our overseas player in 2010.

As of May 2024, Steve had played 109 tests and scored 9,685 runs with 32 centuries, and equally impressive figures in ODI and Twenty 20 International Cricket.

In the 2013 match, the home side replied with 284 all out, D K H Mitchell the Worcestershire captain scoring 65 and N R D Compton 79.

The Australians added 344 for 5 in their second innings, M J Clarke scoring 124 and P J Hughes 86.

The match ended drawn with Worcester 274 for 5. M G Pardoe 57, D H K Mitchell 54 and T C Fell 62 not out.

And so to August 2019, the last First-Class match against a touring side.

Australia were asked to bat first and scored 266 for 5 declared. T M Head making 109 not out, and Usman Khawaja 57.

Travis Head had of course played for Worcestershire during 2018.

Worcestershire replied and declared with 201 for 9 wickets, A G Milton scoring 74 and C A J Morris 53 not out.

Hazlewood and Starc leading the Australian bowling attack.

Australian in their second innings were 124 for 2 at the close of play. M S Harris making 67.

So that may end the unique history of New Road. Not every tour opened at Worcester, but this book compiles the tourist matches, since 1899, and attempts to identify the International Cricketers who walked on to New Road to play their first match in England for their Country. There are probably very few who could say they had not played before the Cathedral in their career and in the next part of this book I will try and identify those unique Stars who did walk down the Pavilion steps full of pride in themselves and for what they might achieve for their Country.

I apologise now if somewhere within this book there are errors. Every care has been taken to research and record the detailed facts but I am sure somewhere, some Scorer in the past missed a vital fact!!

I can only thank them for their diligence in recording First Class Cricket in the detail that they did.

REFERENCES

REFERENCE: INITIAL FIRST MATCH OF THE TOUR

1929 SOUTH AFRICA
1930 AUSTRALIA
1934 AUSTRALIA
1935 SOUTH AFRICA
1936 INDIA
1938 AUSTRALIA
1939 WEST INDIES
1946 INDIA
1947 SOUTH AFRICA
1948 AUSTRALIA
1950 WEST INDIES
1951 SOUTH AFRICA
1952 INDIA
1953 AUSTRALIA
1954 PAKISTAN
1955 SOUTH AFICA
1956 AUSTRALIA
1957 WEST INDIES

1958 NEW ZEALAND
1959 INDIA
1960 SOUTH AFRICA
1961 AUSTRALIA
1962 PAKISTAN
1963 WEST INDIES
1964 AUSTRALIA
1965 NEW ZEALAND
1966 WEST INDIES
1967 INDIA
1968 AUSTRALIA
1971 PAKISTAN
1972 AUSTRALIA
1978 PAKISTAN
1980 WEST INDIES
1982 ZIMBABWE
1984 WEST INDIES
1986 INDIA

1989 AUSTRALIA
1990 NEW ZEALAND
1991 WEST INDIES
1992 PAKISTAN
1993 AUSTRALIA
1994 NEW ZEALAND
1995 WEST INDIES
1996 INDIA
1998 SOUTH AFRICA
1999 NEW ZEALAND
2000 WEST INDIES
2001 AUSTRALIA
2013 AUSTRALIA

1969 WEST INDIES following a first-class match v D H Robins X1.

1973 NEW ZEALAND following a first-class match v D H Robins X1.

1974 PAKISTAN following a first-class match v D H Robins X1.

2003 ZIMBABWE after a first-class match v British Universities.

2004 NEW ZEALAND after a first-class match v British Universities.

FINAL SUMMARY

1929 SOUTH AFRICA.

H B Cameron: Played 26 tests; 1927/28-1935.

C L Vincent: Played 25 tests; 1927/28-1935.

A L Ochse: Played 3 tests; 1927/28-1929.

I J Siedle: Played 18 tests, 1 test century; 1927/28-1935/36.

J A J Christy: Played 10 tests. I test century; 1929-1931/32.

B Mitchell: Played 42 tests, 8 centuries; 1929-1948/49.

N A Quinn: Played 12 tests, 35 wickets; 1929-1931/32.

E L Dalton: Played 15 tests 2 centuries, 12 wickets; 1929-1938/39.

1930 AUSTRALIA

D G Bradman: Played 52 tests, 29 centuries; 1928/29-1948.

V Y Richardson: Played 19 tests 1 test century; 1924/25-1935/36. Grandfather of I M and G S Chappell.

E L a'Beckett: Played 4 tests; 1928/29-1931/32.

A Jackson 8: Played tests, 1 century; 1928/29-1930/31.

A G Fairfax: Played 10 tests, 21 wickets 1928/29-1930/31.

P M Hornibrook: Played 6 tests, 17 wickets; 1928/29-1930.

T W Wall: Played 18 tests 56 wickets; 1928/29-1934.

S J McCabe: Played 39 tests 6 centuries, 36 wickets; 1930-1938.

1931 NEW ZEALAND non-season opener. No debuts.

1932 INDIA non season opener. No debuts.

1933 WEST INDIES non-season opener. No debuts.

1934 AUSTRALIA

W J O'Reilly: Played 27 tests, 144 wickets; 1931/32-1945/46.

E H Bromley: Played 2 tests; 1932/33-1934.

H I Eberling: Played 1 test, 1934.

1935 SOUTH AFRICA

X C Balaskas: Played 9 tests, 1 century. 22 wickets 1930/31-1938/39.

R J Crisp: Played 9 tests, 20 wickets; 935-1935/36.

A D Nourse: Played 34 tests 9 centuries; 1935-1951.

E A B Rowan: Played 26 tests 3 centuries; 1935-1951.

H F Wade: Played 10 tests; 1935-1935/36.

1936 INDIA

S M Hussain: Played 44 tests; 1925/26-1942/43.

L Amarnath: Played 24 tests,1 century, 45 wickets; 1933/34-1952/53.

V M Merchant: Played 10 tests, 3 centuries; 1933/34-1951/52.

S Mushtaq Ali: Played 11 tests 2 centuries; 1933/34-1951/52.

Maharajkumar of Vizianagram: Played 3 tests; 1936.

K R Meherhomji: Played 1 test; 1936.

C Ramaswami: Played 2 tests; 1936

M Baga Jilani: Played 1 test; 1936

1937 NEW ZEALAND. Non-season opener.

1938 AUSTRALIA

J H W Fingleton: Played 18 tests, 5 centuries; 1931/32-1938.

E C S White: Played no tests.

E L McCormick: Played 12 tests, 36 wickets; 1935/36-1938.

C L Badcock: Played 7 tests, 1 century; 1936/37-1938.

A L Hassett: Played 43 tests, 10 centuries;1938-1953.

1939 WEST INDIES

J E D Sealy: Played 11 tests; 1929/30-1939.

G E Gomez: 29 tests, 1 century, 58 wickets; 1939-1954/55.

J B Stollmeyer: Played 32 tests 4 centuries, 13 wickets; 1939-1954/55.

K H Weekes: Played 2 tests, 1 century; 1939.

T F Johnson: Played 1 test; 1939.

1946 INDIA

Gul Mohammad: Played 8 tests for India, 1 test for Pakistan; 1946-1956/57.

M H Mankad: Played 44 Tests, 5 centuries ,162 wickets; 1946-1958/59.

R S Modi: Played 10 tests, 1 century; 1946-1952/53.

S G Shinde: Played 7 tests, 12 wickets; 1946-1952.

C T Sarwate: Played 9 tests, 3 wickets; 1946-1951/52.4.

1947 SOUTH AFRICA

J D Lindsay: Played 3 tests; 1947.

N B F Mann: Played 19 tests, 58 wickets; 1947-1951.

A M B Rowan: Played 15 tests, 54 wickets; 1947-1951.

L T D Tuckett: Played 9 tests. 19 wickets; 1947-1948/49.

D V Dyer: Played 3 tests; 1947.

J B Plimsoll: Played 1 test, 3 wickets; 1947.

D W Begbie: Played 5 tests, 1 wicket; 1948/49-1949/50.

1948 AUSTRALIA

I W G Johnson: Played 45 tests, 109 Wickets; 1945/46-1956/57.

R R Lindwall: Played 61 tests, 2 centuries, 228 wickets; 1945/46-1959/60.

C L McCool: Played 14 tests, 1 century, 36 wickets; 1945/46-1949/50.

D Tallon: Played 21 tests; 1945/46-1953.

E R H Toshack: Played 12 tests, 47 wickets; 1945/46-1948.

A R Morris: Played 46 tests, 12 centuries; 1946/47-1954/55.

1949 NEW ZEALAND

C Burke: Played 1 test, 2 wickets; 1945/46.

F B Smith: Played 4 Tests; 1946/47-1951/52.

J R Reid: Played 58 tests, 6 centuries, 85 wickets; 1949-1965.

J A Hayes: Played 15 tests, 30 wickets; 1950/51-1958.

1950 WEST INDIES

S Ramadhin: Played 43 tests, 158 wickets; 1950-1960/61.

K B Testrall.

J D C Goddard: Played 27 tests, 33 wickets; 1947/48-1957.

P E W Jones: Played 9 tests, 25 wickets; 1947/48-1951/52.

C L Walcott: Played 44 tests, 15 centuries,11 wickets; 1947/48-1959/60.

E D Weekes: Played 48 tests, 15 centuries ;1947/48-1957/58.

F M M Worrell: Played 51 tests, 9 centuries, 69 wickets; 1947/48-1963.

H H H Johnson: Played 3 tests, 13 wickets; 1947/48-1950.

A F Rae: 15 tests, 4 centuries; 1948/49-1952/53.

1951 SOUTH AFRICA

J E Cheetham: Played 24 tests; 1948/49-1955.

M G Melle: Played 7 tests, 26 wickets; 19499/50-1952/53.

G W A Chubb: Played 5 tests, 21 wickets; 1951.

D J Mcglew: Played 34 tests, 7 centuries; 1951-1961/62.

W R Endean: Played 28 tests, 3 centuries; 1951-1957/58.

1952 INDIA

H R Adhikari: Played 21 tests, 1 century, 3 wickets; 1947/48-1958/59.

D G Pradkar: Played 31 tests, 2 centuries, 62 wickets; 1947/48-1958/59.

P K Sen: Played 14 tests; 1947/48-1952/53.

Ghulam Ahmed: Played 22 tests, 68 wickets; 1948/49-1958/59.

P Roy: Played 43 tests, 5 centuries; 1951/52-1960/61.

C D Gopinath: Played 8 tests; 1951/52-1959/60.

G S Ramchand: Played 33 tests, 2 centuries, 41 wickets; 1952/1959/60.

1953 AUSTRALIA

G R Langley: Played 26 tests;1951/52-12956/57.

R Benaud: Played 63 tests, 3 centuries, 248 wickets; 1951/52-1963/64.

C C McDonald: Played 47 tests, 5 centuries; 1951/52-1962.

R G Archer: Played 19 tests, 1 century, 48 wickets; 1952/53-1956/57.

J C Hill: Played 3 tests 8 wickets; 1953-1954/55.

J H De Courcy: Played 3 tests; 1953

1954 PAKISTAN

Ikram Elahi

Shakoor Ahmed.

Fazal Mahmood: Played 34 tests, 139 wickets; 1952/53-1962.

Hanif Mohammad: Played 55 tests, 12 centuries; 1952/53-1969/70.

Waqar Hasan: Played 21tests, 1 century; 1952/53-1959/60.

Mahmood Hussain: Played 27 tests, 68 wickets; 1952/53-1962.

Alimuddin: Played 25 tests, 2 centuries; 1954-1962.

M E Z Ghazali: Played 2 tests; 1954.

Khalid Hasan: Played 1 test, 2 wickets; 1954.

1955 SOUTH AFRICA

T L Goddard: Played 41 tests, 1 century, 123 wickets; 1955-1969/70.

P S Heini: Played 14 tests, 58 wickets; 1955-1961/62.

A R A Murray: Played 1 test, 1 century, 18 wickets; 1952/53-1953/54.

1956 AUSTRALIA

L V Maddocks: Played 7 tests; 1954/55-1956/57.

W P A Crawford: Played, 4 tests, 7 wickets; 1956-1956/57.

K D Mackay: Played 37 tests, 50 wickets; 1956-1962/63.

J W Burke: Played 24 tests, 3 centuries, 8 wickets; 1950/51-1958/59.

1957 WEST INDIES

O G Smith: Played 26 tests, 4 centuries, 48 wickets; 1954/55-1958/59.

D T Dewdney: Played 9 tests, 21 wickets; 1954/55-1957/58.

A G Ganteaume: Played 1 test, I century; 1947/48.

D S Atkinson: Played 22 tests, 1 century, 47 wickets; 1948/49-1957/58.

G S Sobers: Played 93 tests, 26 centuries, 235 wickets; 1953/54-1973/74.

1958 NEW ZEALAND

N S Harford: Played 8 tests; 1955/56-1958.

E C Petrie: Played 14 tests; 1955/56-1965/66.

T Meale: Played 2 tests; 1958.

W R Playle: Played 8 tests; 1958-1962/63.

A R Macgibbon: Played 26 tests, 70 wickets; 1950/51-1958.

A M Moir: Played 17 tests, 28 wickets 1950/51-1958/59.

L S M Miller: Played 13 tests; 1952/53-1958.

1959 INDIA

N S Tamhane: Played 21 tests 1954/55-1960-61

A G Kripal Singh: Played 14 tests, 1 century, 10 wickets; 1955/56-1961/62.

N J Contractor: Played 31 tests, 1 century; 1955/56-1961/62.

C G Borde: Played 55 tests, 5 centuries, 52 wickets; 1958/59-1969/70.

Surendranath: Played 11 tests, 26 wickets; 1958/59-1960/61.

R B Desai: Played 28 tests, 74 wickets; 1958/59-1967/68.

1960 SOUTH AFRICA

A J Pithey: Played 17 tests, 1 century; 1956/57-1964/65.

C Wesley: Played 3 tests; 1960.

J E Pothecary: Played 3 tests 9, wickets; 1960.

A H McKinnon: Played 8 tests, 26 wickets; 1960-1966/67.

1961 AUSTRALIA

I W Quick

A T W Grout: Played 51 tests; 1957/58.

R B Simpson: Played 62 tests, 10 centuries, 71 wickets; 1957/58-1977/78.

R A Gaunt: Played 3 tests, 7 wickets; 1957/58-1963/64.

N C L O'Neill: Played 42 tests, 6 centuries, 17 wickets; 1958/59-1964/65.

F M Misson: Played 5 tests ,16 wickets; 1960/61-1961.

B C Booth: Played 29 tests 5 centuries 3 wickets 1961-1965/66.

1962 PAKISTAN

Haseeb Ahsan: Played 12 tests, 27 wickets; 1957/58-1961/62.

Saeed Ahmed: Played 41 tests, 5 centuries, 22 wickets; 1957/58-1972/73.

Mushtaq Mohammad: Played 57 tests,10 centuries, 79 wickets; 1958/59-1978/79.

Intikhab Alam: Played 47 tests, 1 century, 125 wickets; 1959/60-1976/77.

Mohammad Farooq: Played 7 tests, 21 wickets; 1960/61-1964/65.

Shahid Mahmood: Played 1 test; 1962.

1963 WEST INDIES

E D A S McMorris: Played 13 tests,1 century; 1957/58-1966.

B F Butcher: Played 44 tests, 7 centuries ,5 wickets; 1958/59-1969.

J S Solomon: Played 27 tests 1 century 4 wickets 1958/59-1964/65.

S M Nurse: Played 29 tests, 6 centuries; 1959/60-1968/69.

C C Griffith: Played 28 tests, 94 wickets; 1959/60-1968/69.

D W Allan: Played 5 tests; 1961/62-1966.

1964 AUSTRALIA

N J N Hawke: Played 27 tests, 91 wickets; 1962/63-1968.

T R Veivers: Played 21 tests, 33 wickets; 1963/64-1966/67.

G E Corling: Played 5 tests, 12 wickets; 1964.

R M Cowper: Played 27 tests, 5 centuries, 36 wickets; 1964-1968.

1965 NEW ZEALAND

F J Cameron: Played 19 tests, 62 wickets; 1961/62-1965.

A E Dick: Played 17 tests; 1961/62-1965.

R C Motz: Played 32 tests, 100 wickets; 1961/62-1969.

B W Sinclair: Played 21 tests, 3 centuries; 1962/63-1967/68.

B W Yuile: Played 17 tests, 34 wickets; 1962/63-1969/70.

R O Collinge: Played 35 tests, 116 wickets; 1964/65-1978.

B E Congdon: Played 61 tests, 7 centuries, 59 wickets; 1964/65-1978.

R W Morgan: Played 20 tests, 5 wickets; 1964/65-1971/72.

V Pollard: Played 32 tests, 2 centuries, 40 wickets; 1964/65-1973.

1966 WEST INDIES

J L Hendricks: Played 20 tests; 1961/62-1969

R C Brancker.

1967 INDIA

R F Surti: Played 26 tests, 42 wickets; 1960/61-1969/70.

F M Engineer: Played 46 tests, 2 centuries; 1961/62-1974/75.

D N Sardesai: Played 30 tests, 5 centuries; 1961/62-1972/73.

B S Chandrasekhar: Played 58 tests, 242 wickets; 1963/64-1979.

Hanumant Singh: Played 14 tests, 1 century; 1963/64-1969/70.

S Venkataraghavan: Played 57 tests, 156 wickets; 1964/65-1983/84.

V Subramanya: Played 9 tests, 3 wickets; 1964/65-1967/68.

A L Wadekar: Played 37 tests,1 century; 1966/67-1974

B S Bedi: Played 67 tests, 266 wickets; 1966/67-1979

S Guha: Played 4 tests, 3 wickets; 1967-1969/70

1968 AUSTRALIA. No debuts. No Play

1969 WEST INDIES

G C Shillingford: Played 7 tests, 15 wickets; 1969-1971/72.

V A Holder: Played 40 tests, 109 wickets; 1969-1978/79.

V A Holder had played for Worcestershire throughout 1968, but this was his first appearance representing the West Indies.

1970 No Tour. Rest of the World matches.

1971 PAKISTAN

Aftab Gul: Played 6 tests; 1968/69-1971.

Asif Masood: Played 16 tests, 38 wickets; 1968/69-1976/77.

Zaheer Abbas: Played 78 tests, 12 centuries, 3 wickets; 1969/70-1985/86.

Asmat Rana: Played 1 test; 1979/80.

1972 AUSTRALIA

K R Stackpole: Played 43 tests, 7 centuries, 15 wickets; 1965/66-1973/74.

R W Marsh: Played 96 tests, 3 centuries; 1970/71-1983/84.

D J Colley: Played 3 tests, 6 wickets; 1972.

R AL Massie: Played 6 tests, 31 wickets; 1972-1972/73.

1973 NEW ZEALAND. No debuts

1974 INDIA

S S Naik: Played 3 tests; 1974-1974/75

1975 WORLD CUP.

1976 WEST INDIES. No debuts

1977 AUSTRALIA. No debuts

1978 PAKISTAN

As only 14 overs play was possible, I have only listed one player who actually batted.

Mudassar Nazar 76 tests, 10 centuries, 66 wickets; 1976/77-1988/89.

1978 NEW ZEALAND. No debuts

1979 SRI LANKA. No debuts

1980 WEST INDIES

D L Haynes: Played 116 tests; 18 centuries; 1977/78-1993/94.

D R Parry: Played 12 tests, 23 wickets; 1977/78-1979/80.

S S A F Bacchus: Played 19 tests, 1 century; 1977/78-1981/82.

1981 SRI LANKA and AUSTRALIA. No debuts

1982 ZIMBABWE. Zimbabwe gained test status in 1992.

J G Heron

D A G Fletcher

K M Curran

V R Hogg,

R D Brown

D L Houghton: Played 22 tests, 4 centuries; 1992/93-1997/98.

A J Pycroft: Played 3 tests; 1992/93.

M H E M Dudhia

G M Scott

P W E Rawson.

A J Traicos debut for Zimbabwe but had played 3 tests for South Africa. Played 4 tests for Zimbabwe. 18 wickets; 1969/70-1992/93.

1982 PAKISTAN

Saleem Yousuf: Played 32 tests; 1981/82-1990/91.

1983 NEW ZEALAND. No debuts

1984 WEST INDIES

P J L Dujon: Played 81 tests, 5 centuries; 1981/82-1991.

A L Logie: Played 52 tests, 2 centuries; 1982/83-1991.

R B Richardson: Played 86 tests, 16 centuries; 1983/84-1995.

C A Walsh: Played 132 tests, 519 wickets; 1984/85-2000/01.

1985 AUSTRALIA

G M Ritchie: Played 30 tests, 3 centuries; 1982/83-1986/87.

M J Bennett: Played 3 tests, 6 wickets; 1984/85-85.

D R Gilbert: Played 9 tests, 16 wickets; 1985-1986/87.

R B Phillips.

1986 INDIA

K Srikkanth: Played 43 tests, 2 centuries; 1981/82-1991/92.

Maninder Singh: Played 35 tests ,88 wickets; 1982/83-1992/93.

C Sharma: Played 23 tests, 61 wickets; 1984/85-1988/89.

M Prabakhar: Played 39 tests, 1 century, 96 wickets; 1984/85-1995/96.

M Azharuddin: Played 99 tests, 22 centuries; 1984/85-1999/00.

K S More: Played 49 tests; 1986-1993.

1987 PAKISTAN. No debuts.

1988 WEST INDIES. No debuts.

1989 AUSTRALIA

G R Marsh: Played 50 tests, 4 centuries; 1985/86-1991/92.

M R J Veletta: Played 8 tests; 1987/88-1989/90.

I A Healy: Played 119 tests, 4 centuries; 1988/89-1999/00.

T V Hohns: Played 7 tests, 17 wickets; 1988/89-1989.

M A Taylor: Played 104 tests, 19 centuries; 1988/89-1998/99.

T M Moody: Played 8 tests, 2 centuries, 2 wickets; 1989/90-1992.

1990 NEW ZEALAND

A H Jones: Played 39 tests, 7 centuries; 1986/87-1994/95.

D K Morrison: Played 48 tests, 160 wickets; 1987/88-1996/97.

J P Millmow: Played 5 tests, 4 wickets; 1989/90-1990.

M W Priest: Played 3 tests, 3 wickets; 1990-1998.

1991 WEST INDIES

B C Lara: Played 130 tests, 34 centuries; 1990/91-2006/07.

I B A Allen: Played 2 tests, 5 wickets; 1991.

1992 PAKISTAN

Mushtaq Ahmed: Played 52 tests, 185 wickets; 1989/1990-2003/04.

Aamer Sohail: Played 47 tests, 5 centuries, 25 wickets; 1992-1999/00.

Inzamam-ul-Haq: Played 119 tests, 25 centuries; 1992-2007/08.

Rashid Latif: Played 370 tests, 1 century; 1992-2003/04.

1993 AUSTRALIA

S K Warne: Played 145 tests, 708 wickets; 1991/92-2006/07.

P R Reiffel: Played 35 tests, 104 wickets; 1991/92-1997/98.

B P Julian: Played 7 tests, 15 wickets; 1993-1995/96.

M L Hayden: Played 103 tests, 30 centuries; 1993/94-2008/09.

W J Holdsworth

H T Davis

1994 NEW ZEALAND

B R Hartland: Played 9 tests; 1991/92-1994.

B A Pocock: Played 15 tests; 1993/94- 1997/98.

M N Hart: Played 14 tests, 29 wickets; 1993/94-1995.

H T Davis: Played 5 tests, 17 wickets; 1994-1997/98.

G R Larsen: Played 8 tests, 24 wickets; 1994-1995/96.

1995 WEST INDIES

J C Adams: Played 54 tests, 6 centuries 27 wickets; 1991/92-2000/01.

J R Murray: Played 33 tests, 1 century; 1992/93-2001/02.

S Chanderpaul: Played 164 tests 30 centuries 9 wickets; 1993/94-2014/15.

S C Williams: Played 31 tests, 1 century; 1993/94-2001/02.

R Dhanraj: Played 4 tests, 8 wickets; 1994/95-1995/96.

S L Campbell: Played 52 tests, 4 centuries; 1994/95-2001/02.

1996 INDIA

S C Ganguly: Played 113 tests, 16 centuries 32 wickets;1996-2008/09.

A D Jadeja: Played 15 tests;1992/93-1999/00.

B K V Prasad: Played 33 tests, 96 wickets;1996-2001.

V Rathour: Played 6 tests; 1996-1996/97.

P L Mhambrey: Played 2 tests, 2 wickets;1996.

1996 SOUTH AFRICA A & 1997 PAKISTAN A. No debuts

1998 SOUTH AFRICA

M V Boucher: Played 146 tests, 5 centuries; 1997/98-2011/12.

M Hayward: Played16 tests, 54 wickets; 1999/00-2004.

1999 SRI LANKA A. No debuts

1999 NEW ZEALAND. No play

2000 WEST INDIES

A F G Griffith: Played14 tests, 1 century; 1996/97-2000.

R R Sarwan: Played 87 Tests, 15 centuries, 23 wickets; 1999/00-2011.

C H Gayle: Played 103 tests, 15 centuries, 73 wickets; 1999/00-2014.

W Phillip

M V Nagamootoo: Played 5 tests, 12 wickets; 2000-2002/03.

C D Collymore: Played 30 tests, 93 wickets; 1998/99-2007.

2001 AUSTRALIA

N W Bracken: Played 5 tests, 12 wickets; 2003/04-2005/06.

2002 INDIA. No debuts.

2003 ZIMBABWE

T J Friend: Played 13 tests, 25 wickets; 2001-2003/04.

R W Price: Played 22 tests, 80 Wickets; 1999/00-2012/13.

2004 NEW ZEALAND. No debuts.

2005 AUSTRALIA

B J Haddin: Played 66 tests, 4 centuries; 2008-2015

2013 AUSTRALIA. No debuts.

2019 AUSTRALIA. No debuts.

FINAL NOTES

When I started this book, with its theme in the front of my mind, I really did not know how much research it was going to involve. My thanks go immediately to Cricket Archive who have supplied so much of the detailed information. But it was fascinating to develop the theme, and I hope the reader will be amazed at the great cricketers who first set foot on our square at the County Ground. I accept there are many favourite International Cricketers who debuted elsewhere, but I am sure you will be excited when you read through the constructed list.

In the 21st Century it proved far more difficult to identify debutants as International Cricket changed so much with one day internationals, and other formats.

My aim was from day one to target the initial first-class match. So many of the cricketers mentioned have wonderful One Day International records in more recent years but I felt this book would get so over-run with statistics that I would limit the information given.

Hence in my summary list I merely give the name of each player making their debut at New Road, and details of how many Tests they played for their Country, the number of centuries scores at Test Level and similarly the number of wickets taken and the appropriate dates of their Test Career.

That could have been developed to identify the players who went on to Captain their Country.

For instance, Australia Captains who first played at Worcester were as follows: Vic Richardson, Don Bradman, Lindsay Hassett, Arthur Morris, Ian Johnson, Ray Lindwall, Richie Benaud, Bob Simpson, Brian Booth, and Mark Taylor.

What a pity I could not introduce Steve Smith, who played for Worcestershire in 2010 and went on to captain Australia 109 times and scored 32 test centuries.

So many great Australians who did not play their first match at Worcester.

Neil Harvey, Bill Lawry, Ian Chappell, Greg Chappell, Allan Border, Steve Waugh, Adam Gilchrist, Ricky Ponting, and Michael Clarke, though in one format or other most did grace New Road.

I must also mention Glenn McGrath who played his first match in the UK on 27th May 1997 at Bristol against Gloucestershire, having played his first test match versus New Zealand in November 1993.

Glenn was the second fast bowler to take 500 wickets after Courtney Walsh in Test cricket

The list is similar for the West Indies. I will just mention Frank Worrell, Garfield Sobers, Richie Richardson, Courtney Walsh, Brian Lara, and Jimmy Adams.

Again, I believe Viv Richards played his initial first-class game in May 1976, at Lords against Middlesex.

I leave it to the reader to decide what further information they want about any certain Cricketer or Scorecard.

As to my Interest in Worcestershire County Cricket Club, my first school holiday job was as a Car Park Attendant, with other friends from WRGS. We were paid and 7/6d comes to mind around 1960 (probably per three-day match), but it allowed us to watch a bit of cricket towards close of play. Then we were involved in the evening clean-up of the ground for the next day. Not so onerous when every Corona bottle you found yielded a 2d deposit return at the kiosk.

My profession gave me the opportunity to act for many professional Sportsmen and of course that involved several of our team and many of the overseas players up to the turn of the century.

To serve on the Committee was a great honour and especially as Vice Chairman for four years. It gave me the opportunity to sit and talk to many of my boyhood heroes, and also meet many interesting people who came to watch Cricket away from their expertise.

Doug Ellis and Brain Clough come to mind and of course those occasions when we entertained retired Prime Ministers.

So, Cricket and Worcestershire allowed me to meet so many interesting people from all walks of life and from around the World, but as a final comment in this book, if you asked me who was the most amazing person that I met I will tell you the story.

When I was on the management committee, we decided to have a special lunch with Tom Graveney hosting it. Invites were sent to influential people with a view to seeking sponsorship from their Companies. There were two spaces left the day before and I was asked just to find two interesting people to come along to make the day more interesting.

I asked a friend from our village if he would like to come, as he and his wife had recently returned from Myanmar where his wife had opened a school for the deaf many years before and had found that it was still open despite all the troubles there over the years. I thought he would be interesting, and he asked if he could bring his friend from Ludlow who had recently written a book, so I thought yes that's fine.

Everyone came and sat down to lunch. After an introduction from Tom Graveney everyone took turns to introduce themselves, and it was an impressive gathering. But strangely the little quiet gentleman from Ludlow went last.

There we were all listening, and he said "I am Jimmy James, I was the thirty ninth escapee from Stalag Luft 3 in March 1944. We know it as the Great Escape.

The room was stunned.

Please read Moonless Night by B A Jimmy James, MC RAF.